Perspectives on Applied Christianity

Essays in Honor of Thomas Buford Maston

edited by
William M. Tillman, Jr.

MERCER
UNIVERSITY PRESS

ISBN 0-86554-196-5

Library of Congress Cataloging-in-Publication Data
Main entry under title:
Perspectives on applied Christianity.
    Bibliography: p.
    1. Maston, T. B. (Thomas Buford), 1897–
—Addresses, essays, lectures. 2. Social ethics—
Addresses, essays, lectures.   I. Maston, T. B.
(Thomas Buford), 1897–   .   II. Tillman, William M.
BX6495.M362P46   1986   230'.6132'0924   85-26025
ISBN 0-86554-196-5 (alk. paper)

CONTENTS

EDITORIAL INTRODUCTION

—Give the name of the man who has been called "the conscience of Southern Baptists."

—What man taught at Southwestern Baptist Theological Seminary under all its presidents except its first, B. H. Carroll, and its present one, Russell H. Dilday, Jr.?

If you think these are only possible items for a Southern Baptist Convention trivia game, you have missed their point. Actually, they draw some attention to what should be a part of Southern Baptists' knowledge and understanding of one of their premier teachers, T. B. Maston.

The essays that comprise this issue of *Perspectives in Religious Studies* have been done to honor Dr. Maston. Reflect on these as a composite of a man who has had interests and made contributions in several areas under the rubric of Christian ethics.

Those chosen as writers for this Festschrift are accomplished individuals in their own right. Four of them are former doctoral students of T. B. Maston. Two others are Maston students in a real sense as they have cultivated a professional relationship and friendship over the years with Maston. All these writers share common ground with T. B. Maston in the dedication of their careers and lives to the cause of applied Christianity.

Bob E. Adams, professor of Christian ethics at Seminario Internacional Teologico Bautisto, Buenos Aires, writes of "Maston, Missionaries, and Missions." His somewhat autobiographical account is what could be related by scores of Southern Baptist missionaries. They caught, as much as they were taught, the spirit of Christian missions from T. B. Maston. But, how better to communicate the call of missions?

Further insights into Maston the teacher are given by James Dunn, the Executive Director of the Baptist Joint Committee on Public Affairs in Washington, D. C., who addresses a key area of Maston's research, dialogue, and involvement—the principle of religious liberty and its corollary separation of church and state.

Guy F. Greenfield, professor of Christian ethics at Southwestern Baptist Theological Seminary, considers Maston's hermeneutical approach to the Bible and those implications for continued biblical investigation on the part of Christian ethicists.

Maston may come to mind for more individuals because he has been ever a family man. Much of his writing has addressed the Bible's sayings concerning the various facets of family life. He often refers to the influence of various family members on his perspective of Christian ethics. Julian Bridges, professor of sociology at Hardin-Simmons University, relates this as well and considers further implications of Maston's thought for American family life.

Two other areas in which T. B. Maston has made significant statements are race relations and life-style. John Wood, professor of Christian ethics at Baylor University, reflects on the American black-white racial scene using Maston's perspective as a springboard.

David Wilkinson, director of news and information services for the Southern Baptist Convention Christian Life Commission, deals with life-style. This is possibly the one aspect of applied Christianity about which T. B. Maston has the least in print. Wilkinson's article develops a perspective on life-style sensitive to Maston's thought, as well as to the role model he provides us.

One aspect of Dr. Maston's work that is not given article treatment is his attention to youth and recreation work. Southwestern Seminary, in its early days, was one of the first such institutions to have course work in church recreation. T. B. Maston taught some of those first recreation courses, as well as offerings in social work and student work. His Master of Religious Education thesis, "Reasons for a Church Play Program," and Doctor of Religious Education thesis, "Play Program for the Church," indicate by their titles the interest he had in recreation. Though the course catalog titles do not exactly reflect "Christian ethics," that subject matter was also a part of Dr. Maston's teaching load early in his career.

To aid the reader in gaining a sense of the proportion of T. B. Maston's life, a list of significant dates follows this introduction. In addition, a bibliography of his books is supplied. This is selective because the hundreds of periodical articles, Baptist Sunday School Board curriculum materials, pamphlets, chapter contributions to other authors' books, and audio and video tapes that Maston has done would fill several pages of this publication.

It is characteristic of Dr. Maston that he has some writing project always in the works. He is currently working on a book entitled *Little Words*.

Reading what a man has to say gives one some insight into that man. It is also helpful to read what his interpreters have to say. On those grounds I commend to you the following essays. It has been a privilege to serve as the coordinator of this issue. It has provided an opportunity to retrace T. B. Maston's influences on my own life as well as work with those who did these essays as a ''labor of love.''

William M. Tillman, Jr.

_____

    William M. Tillman, Jr. is assistant professor of Christian ethics at Southwestern Baptist Theological Seminary, Fort Worth, Texas.

THOMAS BUFORD MASTON

1897   Born November 26, Jefferson County, Tennessee

1900   Moved to Union County, Ohio

1904   Entered elementary school at College Corners, Ohio

1911   Moved to Fountain City, Tennessee; graduated from grammar school

1914   Baptized into the Smithwood Baptist Church; felt call into ministry

1916   Graduated from Central High School of Fountain City; licensed to preach; entered Carson-Newman College

1919-1924   Summer worker, Tennessee Baptist Convention

1920   Graduated from Carson-Newman with Essie Mae McDonald; both entered Southwestern Baptist Theological Seminary; both joined Gambrell Street Baptist Church, Forth Worth

1921   Married Essie Mae McDonald, June 11

1922   Began teaching in the School of Religious Education at Southwestern Seminary

1923   Received master of religious education (M.R.E.) degree from Southwestern Seminary; Mrs. Maston taught until 1925

1925   Received doctor of religious education (D.R.E.) degree from Southwestern Seminary; Thomas McDonald Maston born

1927   Ordained as a deacon at Gambrell Street Baptist Church; received master of arts (M.A.) degree from Texas Christian University

1928   Harold Eugene Maston born

1932   Entered Yale University

1937   Published first book—*Handbook for Church Recreation Leaders*

1939   Received doctor of philosophy (Ph.D.) degree from Yale University

1943   Established the Department of Christian Social Ethics at Southwestern Seminary

1946   *Of One* published

1954   Went on speaking tour of mission work in Central and South America

1955   Taught as guest professor at Southern Baptist Theological Seminary

1957   *Christianity and World Issues* published

1959   Taught as guest professor at Southeastern Baptist Theological Seminary; traveled to the Orient speaking at American military bases; published *The Bible and Race* and *Segregation and Desegregation*

1963   Retired from Southwestern Seminary

1966   Taught at the Arab Baptist Seminary in Beirut, Lebanon; received Distinguished award from SBC Christian Life Commission

1967   *Biblical Ethics* published

1969   Taught as guest professor at Golden Gate Baptist Theological Seminary

1971   *The Conscience of a Christian* published

1974   *Why Live the Christian Life?* published

1978   *How to Face Grief* published

1979   Four-week stay in hospital with heart attack

1981   Maston Hall dedicated in honor of Dr. and Mrs. Maston, Gambrell Street Baptist Church

1982   Reprint of *Biblical Ethics* published

1985   Celebrated sixty-fourth wedding anniversary with Mrs. Maston; received Brooks Hayes award, Second Baptist Church, Little Rock, Arkansas

BIBLIOGRAPHY

Maston, T. B. *The Bible and Family Relations*. Nashville: Broadman, 1983. (with William M. Tillman, Jr.)

——————. *The Bible and Race*. Nashville: Broadman Press, 1959.

——————. *Biblical Ethics: A Biblical Survey*. Cleveland: World Publishing Co., 1967. (Republished by Word Books in 1969, and reprinted by Mercer University Press in 1982).

——————. *The Christian and Race Relations*. Memphis TN: Brotherhood Commission, Southern Baptist Convention, n.d.

——————. *The Christian in the Modern World*. Nashville: Broadman Press, 1952.

——————. *Christian Principles and Contemporary Social Problems*. Fort Worth TX: by the author, n.d.

——————. *The Christian, the Church and Contemporary Problems*. Waco TX: Word Books, 1968.

——————. *Christianity and World Issues*. New York: Macmillan Company, 1957.

——————. *The Church and Problems in Family Living*. Fort Worth: Potter's Book Store, 1948.

——————. *The Conscience of a Christian*. Waco TX: Word Books, 1971.

——————. *God Speaks Through Suffering*. Waco TX: Word Books, 1977.

——————. *God's Will and Your Life*. Nashville: Broadman Press, 1964.

——————. *Handbook for Church Recreation Leaders*. Nashville: Sunday School Board, 1937.

——————. *How to Face Grief*. Waco TX: Word Books, 1978.

——————. *Isaac Backus: Pioneer of Religious Liberty*. London: James Clark and Co., 1962.

——————. *"Mommie": A Personal Tribute to Essie Mae McDonald (Mrs. T. B.) Maston*. Fort Worth: Privately published, 1980.

——————. *Of One*. Atlanta: Home Mission Board, 1946.

——————. *Principles of Church Recreation*. Fort Worth TX: Southwestern Mimeographics, n.d.

——————. *Real Life in Christ*. Nashville: Broadman Press, 1974.

_____. *Right or Wrong?* Nashville: Broadman Press, 1955. (Revised edition coauthored with William M. Pinson, Jr., 1971).

_____. *Segregation and Desegregation: A Christian Approach.* New York: Macmillan Co., 1959.

_____. *Suffering: A Personal Perspective.* Nashville: Broadman Press, 1967.

_____. *The Teachings of the Church Concerning the Family and Family Relationships.* Privately published, n.d.

_____. *To Walk as He Walked.* Nashville: Broadman Press, 1985.

_____. *Why Live the Christian Life?* Nashville: Broadman Press, 1974.

_____. *Words of Wisdom.* Nashville: Broadman Press, 1984.

_____. *A World in Travail.* Nashville: Broadman Press, 1954.

MASTON, MISSIONARIES, AND MISSIONS

BOB E. ADAMS
SEMINARIO INTERNACIONAL TEOLOGICO BAUTISTO
BUENOS AIRES, ARGENTINA

INTRODUCTION

Santiago, Chile, lies over a *distant* horizon from Fort Worth, Texas. In the early 1960s, Southern Baptist missionaries from the ''South Field''—Paraguay, Uruguay, Argentina, and Chile—gathered in Santiago to study the Baptist past and peer into a nebulous future. Frank Means, former teacher at Southwestern Baptist Theological Seminary in Fort Worth, and at that time area director for all points in the Western Hemisphere that lay south of the Rio Grande, had called the meeting. The imported spiritual guide for the meeting was a bespectacled, mild-mannered man with an Einsteinesque shock of hair. His slight stature and low voice belied the long shadow and overwhelming influence that he had and would cast on the Southwestern graduates who listened and nodded affirmations as he spoke. They would have added their vocal amen if protocol had permitted. His call was to a responsible, personal renewal of faith in Jesus as the Christ, that would inevitably manifest itself in better relationships with fellow Christians, and would consequentially leaven the Latin society for good and toward justice.

I was present at this meeting in Santiago and if I am to be faithful to my assignment, I must give enough of my background to make understandable clearly both the influence of T. B. Maston on my life and what I believe his influence to be on Southern Baptist missionaries and missions.

A PERSONAL PILGRIMAGE

My cultural heritage is derived purely from Oklahoma and Arkansas, from homesteaders that made the run in the Cherokee Strip and married among the originals, and from Scotch-Irish and English and Dutch migrants that marched, each generation, a little farther south and west from the East Coast to Pike and Clark Counties, Arkansas (some have gone on to that ultimate goal, California). Restless, fiercely independent and individualistic, they had a hard time coming to grips with the end of the individualistic line and the necessity to create, accept, and live in community.

My spiritual heritage is similar—a little Baptist, a little Disciples, a little Methodist, a little Nazarene. I suppose that I could have been any of the last three, but the witness that finally reached me came through the pastor of the Baptist church in Gentry, Arkansas, and when I was baptized in the icy clear waters of Flint Creek near Springtown, I came up a Baptist and have never regretted it. There, in that white frame building on the corner of Main Street heading west from the railroad tracks, community, true Christian community, enveloped me. Only forty years later have I begun to realize the significance and the blessing of those three years, which ended as I left home after finishing high school.

After high school, attending college seemed impossible; so I set out to see and experience the world. I became a bum, but a Christian bum. Rootless, wandering, and wondering, I ended up near the place where the Columbia River enters the Gorge, on the Oregon side. I worked in a place where other rootless wanderers, most long past wondering, were either finishing their days out of sight of family, friends, and perhaps the law; or some, as I, simply worked at physically hard, dangerous jobs to get ''roll'' enough to move on. It was a place of no real community, where no one really looked at his neighbor, but spent most of his time with eyes focused either slightly ahead and mostly down or back furtively over his shoulder. That ''no community'' place, individualistic to the most extreme, stuck in my being. I have never forgotten it nor gotten away from it.

My theological training began in earnest at Central Baptist Theological Seminary on the Kansas side of Kansas City. Here was community in the true ecumenical sense. Central's student body was a mixture of Northern (American) Baptist, Mennonite Brethren, and Southern Baptist, in equal doses.

Central's founding in the early 1900s was a midwestern Baptist response to what was perceived as eastern theological modernism. H. E. Dana, far ahead of his contemporaries in scriptural analysis and warmheartedly contagious in courageous Christian living, had recently given his life, literally, for his two families, physically and spiritually.

W. W. Adams, Jr., succeeded Dana, in the A. T. Robertson-Southern tradition that also fostered a Clarence Jordan and Koinonia Farms. Those of us who studied at Central in those years can never deny how he infected us irreversibly with a perspective on the whole of Christian life and the blessed urgency of living it fully.

Adams was representative of the entire faculty, first among peers who, all together, lived the Gospel in and out of the classroom. When professors took preaching and teaching engagements on the weekends, they voluntarily placed all their honoraria and love gifts, minus traveling expenses, in a common fund that was dipped into to help the needy. I know because I was one of those needy helped, and the only way I can repay that debt is by the same route—Christian community.

One lesson I began learning, although I do not recollect being taught it overtly, was that the Christian life should be such that, when any community member has a need, any need, those who have any means of meeting the need, share. As long as anyone has anything to eat, everyone has something to eat. That was, and is, basic biblical ethics and helped prepare the way for T. B. Maston's direct influence on my life a decade later.

A divine call to missions interrupted graduate studies in a prestigious Southern divinity school. After appointment to Chile, I met T. B. Maston as related in the introduction. This was only the beginning of his influence on me, however.

An involved, circuitous pilgrimage later led me and my wife and three preteen daughters to Southwestern Seminary, where I immersed myself in the formal study of ethics, missions, and philosophy of religion. Although he had retired some years before, Dr. Maston came out of retirement to direct a year-long seminar in biblical ethics. As Adams had influenced me over a decade earlier, Maston began to influence me. Those two men, along with the pastor who baptized me, have shaped my life as have no others. It is my unshakable conviction that their teaching reflects that of the Apostle who wrote, "Imitate me—as long as I imitate Christ!"

Armed with a newly earned doctorate from a beloved seminary, my family and I returned to the mission field. A few years later we had to turn our faces northward once more. My wife was fatally ill. Doors of teaching opportunities opened at New Orleans seminary, and then at Southwestern.

How does one describe our ever-deepening, maturing relationship with Dr. Maston? He was an impactor of mission life, spiritual guide, seminar director (a challengingly tough one, too!), continuing counselor, now mentor (blessed word with special meaning) and through it all, a true friend. A full generation my senior, his comforting hand and calming words brought unutterable consolation during the struggle when my wife, mother of my three daughters, died. I believe that his unwavering support in the years that have followed has helped guide me and Sheri, God's gift as companion and co-laborer, once again into missions.

Any and all evaluation that I shall give of T. B. Maston and his influence on missions and missionaries must be understood from the perspective of involvement—personal, unreserved involvement. As his life and teachings exemplify involvement in the lives of missionaries, there were those whose lives and teachings made an impact on his life.

INFLUENCES ON MASTON

What I shall say now of T. B. Maston is drawn not only from the writings that he has done so well, but also, and primarily, from conversations in his office, in his home, and in the car going from place to place. In point of time, his first and strongest influence was his father, a hardworking East Tennessean. (Those not familiar with Tennessee need to know that it is a divided state: West, Middle, and East, and that when Tennessee seceded from the Union at the beginning of The War, East Tennessee in turn seceded from Tennessee.) Hard work, frugality, fierce honesty and independence, shot through with an indomitable Christian faith formed the legacy from those East Tennessee parents. Although T. B. Maston has lived his adult life far from the Smokies, he has never strayed from his heritage, neither in life nor in teaching.

Next, in point of time only, is the influence of "Mommie," his wife for more than sixty years. As the later years have advanced, so has his expressed dependence on and confidence in "Mommie." In very real, even tangible, ways they have learned from and through each other. One of his best writings is a little-known and moving tribute to the woman whose life he has shared since shortly after leaving the East Tennessee mountains. Surely it can be said that they have become that "one flesh" of which the Bible speaks so often. This is so true that to speak of or know T. B. Maston is to speak of and know "Mommie." She is there, in all his writing and speaking. Her loyalty to and participation in their church, Gambrell Street in Fort Worth, is matched and complemented by his.

A third influence on T. B. Maston has been that of their two sons, "Tom Mac" and Gene. As I have observed and become somewhat a part of family through the years, I have come to understand that their influence is dialectical. Tom Mac is brain-damaged, something that probably happened during birth. He has been completely physically dependent all his life, as much now at past middle-age as he was at six months. The Mastons may have at one time seriously considered institutionalizing him, but they have willingly and gladly accepted caring for him. Tom Mac has brought into their lives agonizing questions—"Why?", "For what purpose?", "How long?", and possibly "Why us?"—questions for which there are no satisfactory answers in this life. Their response, however, is the answer: an unquestioning faith in God's abiding presence, and a willingness to learn and share. I have never fully known and always wonder how I would have functioned as the younger son, Gene. The time and effort spent in caring for Tom Mac surely could have been interpreted, at times, as favoritism, and his reaction could have been negative. Human beings have never been granted more than twenty-four hours a day, and can only be present physically in one place at a time. A decision to be here to do this means not to be there and do that. I believe that this kind of existential decision guided T. B. Maston, however consciously or subconsciously, in his ministry outside their home, and to which I shall return later.

A fourth influence on T. B. Maston was the totality of his stay at Yale. Tom Mac and Gene were very young. He already had an advanced degree from Southwestern, but his move into the discipline of ethics called for technical training in the field, hence Yale and H. Richard Niebuhr. Richard Niebuhr's influence on Christian ethicists in the United States, and through him that of Ernst Troeltsch, is really incalculable. Since Maston did not write for publication until after his graduate work at Yale, it is difficult to assess exactly what that influence meant to him personally. However, I believe that his tacit acceptance of Niebuhr's "Christ transforming culture" perspective, with Mastonian alterations, can be traced in his writings and in his teaching. More of this will come later, as I believe it to be of major importance as Maston has influenced Baptist missionaries and missions.

I cannot date a fifth influence on Maston. It likely was a growing perception. An ethicist would call it "natural law ethics," and it involves a way of perceiving or conceiving the world (read, universe) as it relates to God. In this perspective, God created the world to function according to certain laws, and it does indeed function according to them. These laws are both physical and moral. Consequently, any observing individual can, by studying carefully the way the world functions, discover both the physical and moral laws by which it operates, and govern his life accordingly. The God of moral and physcial law in creation is also the God who reveals himself most completely through Scripture and in Scripture through Christ. I think that this emphasis, clear in Maston, perhaps derives from reflection on Tom Mac in their lives and on the experience that I describe next.

While Maston was at Yale he became seriously ill. According to his own evaluation, he was as close to dying as one can be and yet recover. He is convinced that his recovery was due to the direct intervention of God, that from his recovery on he has been a "marked man," and that his ministry has been in a real sense payment for an unrepayable debt—the gift of life. He transmitted his sense of urgency to his pupils. With and within him at all times has been a deep sense of urgency, humility, and gratitude. At least, the first his pupils have unhesitatingly demonstrated, if not always the second and third.

MASTON'S INFLUENCE

The students I mention are typical of those Maston has. That may be part of the reason why I cannot list them all, for they are too numerous. But, representatively they are: Jase Jones, a longtime worker in Interfaith Witness for the Home Mission Board, retired, but no less active; Keith Wills, recently retired librarian at Southwestern Seminary and mission volunteer worker; Jimmy Allen, currently director of the Baptist Radio and Television Commission; Foy Valentine, director of the Southern Baptist Christian Life Commission; James Dunn, director of the Baptist Joint Committee on Public Affairs; James Giles, director of the Baptist Seminary in Cali, Colombia; Julian Bridges, then-missionary, now professor at Hardin-Simmons University; C. W. Scudder, Maston colleague at Southwestern and later administrator/teacher at Midwestern Seminary; John Howell, longtime ethics professor at Midwestern; Bill Pinson, Maston colleague at Southwestern, now executive secretary of the Texas Baptist Convention; Ebbie Smith, then-missionary and now professor of ethics and missions at Southwestern Seminary, along with Guy Greenfield, professor of ethics also at Southwestern.

The list could go on. These are only a sampling of the many who did doctoral work with Maston. How many scores of others sat in his classes, read his books, completed his assignments? Only the computer could tell us.

Then there have been the years past retirement, more than two decades. At the beginning of this time I came under his influence. It would not be an overstatement to say that I fell under his spell; for such it is. For years he was a regular at the orientation sessions for career missionaries sent out by the Foreign Mission Board of the Southern Baptist Convention. Southern Baptists also have a two-year missions track for young adults, called the Journeyman Program. From the inception of the program T. B. Maston has not only been a regular, but I can vouch that he is always the favorite personality at Journeyman orientation. I have seen him, advanced in years, sit in an easy chair with young Baptist adults seated round on the floor, listening, literally for hours, as he taught of personal responsibility in the Christian life.

One of his many books, *Right or Wrong,* has been translated and used in many areas of the world. His lecture notes from the basic ethics course have been transformed and translated by James Giles into *Bases Bíblicas de la Etica,* and the book is used throughout the Spanish-speaking world. It is quoted extensively in a work on Christian ethics written by a Spaniard for use primarily in Spain. For a book written in Latin American Spanish to be used extensively and appreciatively in Spain is an ultimate compliment.

Impressionistically but none the less valuable, I have heard repeatedly comments by missionaries on the field and on furlough, about the influence Dr. Maston had on them. It is always difficult for one teacher to leave an unforgettable, indelible impression during that three-year whirlwind of exposures-to-material (we hope that at least some real learning takes place) called seminary training. Biblical studies and languages, homiletics, missions, evangelism, church history, pastoral ministry, and the systematic disciplines of theology, philosophy of religion and ethics must all be studied in three years. Many have testified that Maston helped them "put it together," and that is a compliment.

EVALUATION

Where would Southern Baptist missions and missionaries be without Maston? Obviously, there have been and are other influential, solid ethicists that have contributed through their seminaries, as Maston did through his. But I speak of Southwestern and Southwesterners, not in any boastful but in a grateful sense: grateful for him and grateful for all them. I want to write of Maston's positive and lasting contributions, and how we, who have been influenced by him, can best continue what he helped begin in us.

First, his own rugged individualism reflects and is reflected in the concept of the priesthood of the believer. For a Baptist, this means every person is his/her own priest—no intermediaries, but direct contact with God. Not a total mysticism, for Bible and Christian friends are there and real. However, both first and last, no one stands between God and the individual, particularly in matters of decision making: "What should I do," or, "What do I do?" No one else can answer for me. This call and emphasis on personal responsibility rings true again and again in everything T. B. Maston has said, written, and done.

Second, he placed emphasis on and appreciated the family. Here is where his own immediate experience and biblical emphases converge, and here is where he has been of great help in the lives of missionaries, particularly in orientation sessions in the United States prior to mission service and on the field in the midst of pressures unimagined in the homeland.

Third, he insisted that true Christian ministry invariably creates tension. It is a tension that begins in the individual Christian, a tension between what and whom he knows himself to be and what and whom he knows he should be. This tension, actualized in the ministry of the individual, is also felt in the larger society, as it acknowledges what it is and realizes what it could and should be.

Fourth, he relied, at times overt, but always present, on a concept of natural law in ethics that seems to derive from natural law in physics and biology. Due to his obvious, continuing insistence on both Scripture interpretation and a kind of mysticism to arrive at valid ethical decisions, this reliance on natural law concepts is difficult to trace and place in context.

Fifth, he had final, complete, utter dependence on God, practically unmediated and direct. This influence comes full circle and is intimately related to the first. Part of the circle is his conviction that God most completely revealed himself and his will in the Bible, and there most fully in the person of Jesus of Nazareth. To depend on the Bible, as it is rightly understood, is for T. B. Maston to depend on God.

Two problems have arisen, consistently and insistently, for me as a disciple of Maston. One reason for the rather lengthy autobiographical excursus is to offer the reader an opportunity to evaluate whether these problems arise from my own pilgrimage alone, or whether they arise from Maston's influence, or perhaps from both. I believe that I can see at least reflections of these same problems in other disciples, so I suspect that they derive at least in some way from his influence on us.

The first problem has to do with the concept of natural law. Ernst Troeltsch is not, perhaps, the best interpreter of Baptists, particularly Southern Baptists. He did not know us firsthand but he did know continental and British Baptists, and also seemed in the latter years of his life to be drawn toward their outlook on the Christian life and its relationship to the world. He believed that one distinguishing characteristic of Baptists was their rejection of the concept related to ethics. Indeed, he seemed to believe that it was this rejection that helped form what he called the ''sect'' (*gruppen*) mentality. (I have some problem with translating *gruppen* by ''sect.'')

The notion that universally observable and understandable natural moral law has a legitimate place in Christian ethics raises for me, the specter of coercion, if not in matters of belief, at least in matters of behavior. I think I see a positive sanction for coercion inherent in the concept. If this is true, there is a grave problem if not contradiction, if not between the concept of the priesthood of the believer and the concept of natural law, then between a corollary of the concept of priesthood of the believer, that of a gathered, voluntaristic church and the concept of natural law.

Maston seems nowhere to draw the social conclusions of his concept of natural law, so we do not know how he would resolve this very real problem. There are immediate consequences for missions. To the extent that one is a ''natural law'' ethicist he/she should raise the question of coercion. To the extent that one is not, he/she should raise the question of how to relate to the coercive facet of every nonvoluntaristic society. Maston seems to lean heavily on the side of nonresistance to what would be interpreted by Christians as nonjustifiable coercion.

This question leads me to another, inextricably related to the first, concerning the nature and function of church, as this is part of the life of the individual Christian and as it is situated in the larger context of other communities. To Maston (and to me) church is a voluntaristic community, an idea that flows ineluctably from the concept of the priesthood of the believer. But the concept of priesthood of the believer is a two-edged sword. Paradoxically, although it first means that one is his/her own priest, it also means that one is, to some extent, priest to his/her brother/sister in Christ in community. One ''volunteers,'' but for what? What is the function of the community into which one has volunteered? I believe that the biblical concept is that of a disciplined, disciplinary, intradisciplining community. To be sure, one could ''volunteer out'' just as one ''volunteered in,'' and this has tremendous theological implications. However, I am thinking more of the individual's decision-making process, and questioning whether it really is as individualistic as Maston understands it. In Scripture, both Old and New Testaments, the People of God, the Community of God, the *Qahal,* the *Ecclesia,* are primary (in the sociological sense) and thus former and informers of the individual's conscience and decision making. Without deprecating in any way either the priesthood of the believer or the church as voluntary community, I become more convinced, as I see struggling, divided and divisive Baptist churches, true minority groupings on the mission field, that we need to reexamine the concept of church as conscience-shaper and informer of the individual believer, with the believer an active, *never* passive, part of the shaping and informing process.

CONCLUSION

The reader will miss the intent of these latter paragraphs if they are read as overly negative about the ramifications of some of T. B. Maston's thought. Rather, those of us whose lives have been shaped and molded by this slightly built giant will be remiss in our gratitude to him and in our responsibility to our Lord if we do not take what he has so freely given and build on it creatively and responsibly.

THE CHRISTIAN AND THE STATE: A CONSTRUCTIVE TASK

JAMES M. DUNN
BAPTIST JOINT COMMITTEE ON PUBLIC AFFAIRS
WASHINGTON DC

INTRODUCTION

"One cannot be a good Christian without being a good citizen." More than once T. B. Maston has made that statement: atypical for him, sweeping and categorical, shocking to those of his students who had never thought that citizenship had anything to do with their religion.

Several presuppositions lurk behind this stark axiom:

God cares about the affairs of state.
Good citizenship can be discerned and deliberately engaged.
A difference exists between Christianity and citizenship.
A moral measure can and should be taken in the political realm of life.
One makes ethical choices, both political and religious.

One could stretch these pedagogic proverbs too far, but they do reveal a dimension of Maston's thought.

BEING LIGHT AND LEAVEN

Thomas Buford Maston's political ethic, especially in his focus on church-state relations, is a disproportionately significant aspect of his contribution. In fact, his political ethic reflects, if it does not determine, that which is most distinctive in the Maston ethic.

Isaac Backus: Pioneer of Religious Liberty[1] is an abridgement of Maston's doctoral dissertation at Yale University. The Southwestern ethicist identifies closely with Backus. He stands with Backus, a dissenter, and clings to the noble train of Baptist dissent. He admires and emulates Isaac Backus as a prolific writer who addressed the issues of his day forthrightly. Finally, the one phase of Backus's thought and work that Maston gives the most attention was his "political ethic with its emphasis on liberty of conscience."[2]

MULTIPLYING INFLUENCE

The doctoral students in Southern Baptist seminaries by one count turned out 143 dissertations related to Christian social ethics from the first such product in 1894 through 1966 when the last of Maston's "boys" completed his work. Of these, forty-eight (over a third) were the work of Maston students. More pertinent, perhaps, is the heavy political concentration in dissertation titles from Southwestern Seminary, Maston's turf.

Maston's protégés wrote on: Southern Baptist attitudes toward church-state cooperation in religious instruction; Southern Baptist reactions to diplomatic relations with the Vatican (1939-1953); Southern Baptists and the relationship of church and state (1918-1952); Contemporary Southern Baptist involvement with the state; and Southern Baptists and labor.

In addition, of fourteen dissertations from the ethics department at Southwestern that explored the ethical thought of individuals, four of them dealt with the Niebuhrs, two with Rauschenbusch. Others examined political ethicists and champions of liberty including Harry Emerson Fosdick, E. Stanley Jones, George W. Truett, John Bunyan, and J. M. Dawson.

A dozen doctoral scholars delivered dissertations on subjects not specifically political but touching the realm of church-state concerns. They wrote about social action, the social gospel, a Christian approach to community life, economic injustice, capital punishment, war and peace, collectivism, freedom (the focus of two studies) and race relations (theme for three dissertations).[3]

PUBLIC POLICY AND CHRISTIANS

Another evidence of Maston's concern for the church-state question is his recurring appeal to the centrality of public policy as a proper subject for

---

[1]T. B. Maston, *Isaac Backus: Pioneer of Religious Liberty* (London: James Clarke & Company Ltd.) 3.

[2]Ibid., 6.

[3]"Doctoral Dissertations Relative to Christian Social Ethics," an unpublished paper.

Christian ethics. He has a high view of democracy and sees it closely linked to Christianity. "It is doubtful if there is a sound basis for political democracy where there is lacking a vital Christian movement."[4]

"It would be tragic to the democratic movement for its leaders to forget its vital historic relation to the Christian faith,"[5] Maston contends. Yet, he, unlike the "Christian nation" theocrats, has known all along that "it would be a mistake to claim that democracy stems entirely from Christianity."[6]

T. B. Maston has never fallen into the trap of identifying his country and its political system with God's plan and people. He consistently has denied the "identification" theory as the proper relation of church and state.[7] The popular idea in the 1980s that the United States of America somehow has an extension of a covenant arrangement worked out by God as a special nation is a notion foreign to Maston. "Christians should never go so far as to identify the Christian movement with any particular political system,"[8] he says. He fears a civil religion that equates our culture with the kingdom of God.

Into this incipient political framework Maston throws a plea for active participation in the political process. He insists that "one of the chief threats to political democracy is the poor citizenship of good people,"[9] that "the Christian religion needs to permeate every phase of life,"[10] and that "one of the greatest responsibilities of the individual is to accept the responsibility of freedom."[11]

The professor holds a high view of democracy and pushes for the practice thereof. He sees "democracy as government by discussion (with) . . . decisions by persuasion and arbitration."[12] He warns that the "rights of the minority will not and cannot be properly protected unless there is freedom of speech, press and assembly."[13] He insists that "another characteristic of de-

---

[4]T. B. Maston, *The Christian, the Church, and Contemporary Problems* (Waco TX: Word Books, Publishers) 206.

[5]T. B. Maston, *The Christian in the Modern World* (Nashville TN: Broadman Press) 96-97.

[6]Ibid., 96.

[7]Ibid., 94.

[8]Ibid., 96.

[9]Maston, *The Christian, the Church, and Contemporary Problems*, 208.

[10]T. B. Maston, "The Church, the State and the Christian Ethic," *Journal of Church and State* 2 (May 1960): 28.

[11]Ibid., 31.

[12]Maston, *The Christian, the Church, and Contemporary Problems*, 203.

[13]Ibid., 204.

mocracy is that it is an open rather than a closed society. The people have an opportunity to know about failures as well as successes."[14]

So, Maston in no sense counsels withdrawal from the world, hatred for dirty politics, or turning to individualistic piety or spiritual strategies. He understands that religion and politics will mix, must mix, ought to mix, especially in a democracy.

ACTIVISM AND ACADEMICS

The professor has trained activists but has never completely escaped academe in his understanding of how politics work "in the trenches." He still advises nonpartisan purity for Christian citizens. Wisely he cautions that one "should maintain his independence of machine or party control,"[15] but unrealistically he suggests that "all who do participate publicly should restrict themselves to principles and programs, guarding against dealing in personalities."[16]

Those of his graduate students who have moved most actively into the political process and the ones who have worked out the principles he emphasized have not followed his advice "that the vast majority of Christians should be politically independent." Practitioners deny the argument that "by being an independent, they can best make their influence felt in the political world."[17] That is not the way it works.

THEOLOGICAL UNDERPINNINGS

Maston argues powerfully for political involvement on theological premises. Love of persons demands it. The pursuit of justice requires it. The stewardship of influence cannot be exercised without practiced citizenship. Morality and decency make political decisions necessary. T. B. Maston cannot countenance the silliness that tries to equate "separation of church and state" with separation of religion from politics. The belief that engaging in the public policy debate is off limits for religious persons is the antithesis of the democratic vision. Yet, the Southwestern professor claims the historic Baptist belief in the separation of church and state. One contends that he advances and enhances that claim. He brings fresh insights and a new dyna-

[14]Ibid., 205.

[15]Maston, *The Christian in the Modern World*, 92.

[16]Ibid., 93.

[17]T. B. Maston, *The Conscience of a Christian* (Waco TX: Word Books, Publishers) 133.

mism to church-state separation as a corollary to the affirmation of religious liberty.

Ahead of his time, in the 1950s, T. B. Maston saw the delicate relationship between church and state as one of the crucial issues of the era. He wrote, "The present period is witnessing an unusually acute struggle between these institutions, a struggle that is a world-wide phenomenon."[18] The recent history of Nigeria, Iran, Lebanon, Northern Ireland, Sri Lanka, and events in the United States prove his foresight.

A biblical ethic informs the origin and nature of these basic institutions and casts the limits of their authority. The state "came from God" whether "its authority was a part of God's original purpose" or "was a result of and a remedy for sin."[19]

A theology for religious freedom is rooted in the "viewpoint of the Christian ethic . . . that man was created in the image of God."[20] All freedom, then, is from God. Human beings made like God are able to respond to God, response able, responsible and necessarily free. Without freedom responsibility is a mockery of persons as dumb things. Without responsibility freedom is meaningless, directionless anarchy without accountability.

Church and state are both divine-human institutions, ordained by God, both lifted to the heights and limited by humanity. Both church and state are ennobled and afflicted with mortals that offer stumbling, sinful lives and sometimes heavenly aspirations.

The value of the individual, related directly to being made in the divine image, calls for freedom, dignity and access to the Eternal unimpeded and unsullied by institutions, creeds or any sort of intervention. "Because of his worth and because of the inalienable natural rights that are his, man is to be treated with respect by his fellow man and also by the State and the Church. He is never to be used as a mere instrument or tool."[21]

Because of the universal tendency to sin, because of the inevitable involvement in the sin of the world and because the will of God is not mediated to the individual by the church or the state these institutions are rightly kept separate.

"Separation does not . . . mean that the church or the state ignores the other. Separation of church and state simply means an organizational and a functional separation. . . . It is not a separation of religion and political life.

---

[18]T. B. Maston, *Christianity and World Issues* (New York: The Macmillan Company) 204.

[19]Maston, "The Church, the State, and the Christian Ethic," 28.

[20]Ibid., 29.

[21]Ibid., 31.

Christian principles should be applied to governmental affairs . . . neither the church nor the state should seek to control the other or to use the other to promote its interests."[22]

In the teamwork of the two divinely ordained institutions each plays a distinct role. "The Church is to be a source of strength and encouragement to its members, but in relation to the State it is to serve as a watchman. It is to warn the State against the transgression of its legitimate limits."[23]

Backus said it well: "No man can be made a member of a truly religious society by force, or without his own consent; neither can any corporation that is not a religious society have a just right to govern in religious affairs."[24] Maston agrees with Backus on the idea "that religion is a matter between God and the individual (and) 'will remain an immutable verity as long as Christianity endures.' "[25]

Church-state separation as a safeguard for liberty is for Maston more than an important aspect of the social contract. Separation transcends the rule of law and constitutional theory. The separation is far more than political arrangement open to adjustment by majority vote. "God has not only seen fit to place limits on the authority of both the church and the state; he also places some limits on the rights of the people. They do not have the right to delegate either to the state or to the church the authority to control, or to attempt to control, the consciences of individuals."[26] Maston sings Isaac Watt's song.

> Let Caesar's due be ever paid;
>   To Caesar and his throne;
> But consciences and souls were made
>   To be the Lord's alone.[27]

One sees a distinctive contribution in the political ethic of T. B. Maston. He favors mixing politics and religion without merging church and state. He brings a biblical theology and the discipline of Christian social ethics to bear on the political process. One sees in this his greatest gift to Baptist politics. He modestly advanced his approach. "The study of Church and State may be approached from many different viewpoints. One that is seldom used, and yet one that can be rather fruitful, is from the perspective of the Christian ethic."[28]

---

[22]Maston, *Christianity and World Issues,* 223.

[23]T. B. Maston, *Biblical Ethics* (Cleveland: The World Publishing Company) 240.

[24]Maston, *Isaac Backus,* 78-79.

[25]Ibid., 79.

[26]Maston, *Christianity and World Issues,* 214.

[27]Maston, *The Christian in the Modern World,* 98.

[28]Maston, "The Church, the State, and the Christian Ethic," 26.

METHODOLOGICAL UNDERPINNINGS

Dyadic Style

Julian Bridges suggests that "One distinctive of T. B. Maston's writing is his dyadic-type thinking. Examples of this emphasis are his frequent discussions of such topics as personal and social ethics, positive and negative morality, evangelism and social concern, worship and service, and decisions regarding right and wrong."[29] In Maston's discussion of the needs of individuals and the nature of Church and State one sees the trait that Bridges points out. "This *dependence upon* and yet *independence of* the *Church* and *State* and other institutions stem from the *transcendental-earthly* nature of man. He is *a part of* the natural order, but being created in the image of God he stands *apart from* and above that order."[30] (Emphasis added to the dyads.)

The dyadic thinking of Maston is related to the parallelisms of Hebrew thought and the creative "third options" set out so often by Jesus when he was offered two unacceptable alternatives. Maston's dyads may be more related to commonsense prudence and practical wisdom than to the dialectical thinking of Niebuhr and his mentors. Yet, T. B. Maston demonstrates great talent at eclecticism. He brings sophisticated thought processes within reach without making his students feel foolish.

Maston's favorite test questions began: "Compare and contrast" followed by the most unlikely pairings. He matched the simple and the complex. He seemed to literally feel the current between positive and negative poles. He constantly held in balance the real and the ideal or the realistic and the idealistic. For instance, "when defending democracy, Christian workers should make a clear distinction between the *democratic ideal* and *the democracies.*"[31]

Before it was fashionable he cast much of his lecture material in a prescient awareness of "the already but not yet." Dr. Maston was constantly aware of the conflict between the group or institution and the individual. Professor Bridges sees this balancing act as central to Maston's contribution.

In the areas of Christian citizenship and political participation, Maston's readers soon become aware of a desire on his part to strike a balance between opposites or counterparts of a common theme. Conservatism and lib-

---

[29]William M. Pinson, ed., *An Approach to Christian Ethics* (Nashville TN: Broadman Press) 140.

[30]Maston, "The Church, the State, and the Christian Ethic," 32.

[31]Maston, *The Christian in the Modern World*, 97.

eralism, civil obedience and disobedience, order and justice, local and state responsibilities, national and international commitments, and the relationship between church and state—all of these and other topics are dealt with effectively by suggesting that both parts of the dyad should always be kept under consideration. Neither should be neglected completely, and, where necessary, conciliation rather than conflict should be the dominant, overriding theme.[32]

Citizenship and Compromise

Directly related to this style, this balanced teaching approach is Maston's willingness to accept compromise as the stuff of politics and shift accordingly. Compromise may be the milk of progress and the building blocks of reconciliation in a warring world. "Compromise," he wrote, "does not do any serious damage to the integrity of an individual or a group so long as the end attained is greater or more significant than the sacrifice that was made."[33]

Maston speaks freely of the necessity of accommodation and applauds an accommodative social ethic that does not lose sight of the ideal, that does not equate the compromise with the goal. This sort of social ethic is peculiarly compatible with an ethic for church-state relations.

Creative Tension

"Creative tension" between the dimensions of the dyad is one of the most memorable, universally useful, and clearly characteristic of Maston teaching techniques. Repeatedly, he helps one to see the "other side" of an issue, concept, or ethical emphasis. When one is willing to analyze any moral or ethical problem with Maston he identifies at least for the sake of argument, two or more perspectives or values. Then, the dynamic nature of ethics is invoked and the tension recognized. When those tensions are between competing goods, between the doable and the goal, between the real and the ideal, he appeals to creative tension.

For thousands of students not accustomed to abstractions he likens that creative tension to the pressure on a rubber band, stretched to accomplish its purpose but not stretched to the breaking point. He sees the various strategies of the church in the world like someone who would move a chair. The chair cannot be moved if that someone sits in it placing all his weight on that which he would move. The church is useless when it identifies totally with the culture. Neither can the chair be moved if the someone refuses to touch it. The

---

[32]Pinson, *An Approach to Christian Ethics*.

[33]T. B. Maston, "Ethical Issues 1978 and Beyond" (Nashville: Christian Life Commission of the Southern Baptist Convention).

totally withdrawn church is not worth much. The church is in a posture for world changing when it is in touch but not at rest.

A lively Christian ethic emerges informed by biblical revelation but dependent upon the work of the Holy Spirit. An eclectic ethic comes from Maston consistent internally, conservative theologically, sensitive socially, and workable politically.

Maston's approach to social ethics allows for the divine-human nature of the church and the Bible. His creative tension concept accepts the burden of unresolved problems, unanswered questions. His biblical theology makes for a humble and unpretentious ethic. How foreign to an expanding, vital ethic like his is the triumphal, judgmental morality of Fundamentalism! An orgy of certainty, a letter-of-the-law legalism like that popular in evangelical and Baptist circles in the 1980s does not remotely resemble the T. B. Maston social ethic.

Conflicts and disagreements arise and will continue to arise regarding politics and religion, and church and state. An ethic such as Maston's provides a framework for facing them. With some thorny religio-political puzzles the best for which we can hope is to learn to cope. Many of those church-state issues one would like to settle once and for all will never be put to rest. Maston helps one handle that unwelcome fact.

ISSUES AND IMPLICATIONS

Some of the church-state issues that are in the daily news in the mid-1980s have been responsibly confronted by T. B. Maston early and often in his writing years. Since the 1940s he has dealt consistently and prophetically with troublesome themes. A few of those recurring issues follow.

Secular Humanism

Anxiety about "secular humanism" is not new. In the 1950s Dr. Maston advised that "it is wise for the defenders of separation to recognize the dangers of what is termed secularism, the danger that all of life will be organized as if God did not exist."[34] Yet, he saw a free church in a free state with genuine separation of church and state. He saw "secularism . . . more likely to thrive where there is an established church."[35]

"The threat of secularism to liberty and to the church and its freedom is particularly acute when and where it has become a religion."[36] These words

---

[34]Maston, *Christianity and World Issues*, 224.

[35]Ibid.

[36]Maston, *The Christian, the Church, and Contemporary Problems*, 194.

of T. B. Maston in 1968 were a forewarning of the furor faced today. John C. Bennett suggested in *Christians and the State* that secularist religion became a threat "as it developed a pretentious ideology that offered its own answers to religious questions."[37]

Maston challenges "a more insidious and hence more dangerous threat to religious liberty (that) comes from secularism within our churches."[38] We have, he feels, church members only slightly less secularized than the public that is at odds with the church. The church itself is little less secularized than the culture surrounding it. "Many of our churches identify with and have become defenders of the culture,"[39] Maston laments.

Church leaders decry any civil disobedience for conscience's sake. Pastors act as if they are the CEO of a corporation. Deacons actually see themselves as the "governing board." The modest meetinghouse has become the "church plant."

Maston presciently wrote:

The secularization of the church expresses itself in various and even contradictory ways. The church uses, to a distressing degree, secular methods to attain worldly success. The greatness of a local church is frequently measured by the number of its members, the improvement of its physical facilities, and the size of its budget. One result of this kind of emphasis is that there are evidently many unredeemed people in our churches, with the rest of us considerably less mature than we should be. In turn, the unredeemed and the immature are a constant threat to religious liberty in the world and in the church. There can be no assurance of the preservation of religious liberty in our nation apart from churches composed of redeemed, spiritually maturing men and women who will defend the right and accept the responsibility of religious liberty.[40]

Long before the present hand-wringing about "secular humanism" Maston saw that the real problem is the secularization of the churches. The drive for success, status, size, and fame infects the religion of Jesus Christ.

It is expected in many churches, particularly the larger, "more successful ones," that every recommendation from the pastor, deacons, or any committee will be accepted without any questions. There is little liberty to differ, at least publicly. Religious liberty is largely lost within the house of her

---

[37]John C. Bennett, *Christians and the State* (New York: Charles Scribner's Sons) 238.
[38]Maston, *The Christian, the Church, and Contemporary Problems*, 195.
[39]Ibid.
[40]Ibid.

"friends." How can we expect to preserve it in the nation and the world if we do not preserve it within the company of the redeemed?[41]

Why should churches that are no different from their culture care about maintaining the freedom to critique society? Why should anyone give to a church that seems to be interested only in self-perpetuation? How can one expect spiritual strength from a church that is dedicated to the "bottom line" mentality of our age?

"Some churches with fine buildings have attempted to domesticate God. They tend to be self-centered and in love with themselves,"[42] Maston charges. He sees, correctly, that the most powerful engine in the push toward secularism is the secularization of the churches. How ironic that many who express such fears of secular humanism are precisely the most "show biz" pastors, the most success-oriented churches, the most clergy-dominated fellowships, the most creedal, freedom-denying theologians, the most big-business-defending pawns of politicians, the most statistically sensitive materialists in the religion game.

Years ago T. B. Maston was prophetically speaking out against the secular credo of success. He saw clearly that the desire for secular success "posits a real threat not only to religious liberty but also to the vitality of the Christian movement."[43]

Maston's entire approach to Christian ethics was peculiarly suited to Baptists. He has never accepted unquestioningly the traditional approaches, rather, he fashioned a practical, political, philosophical, biblical approach to the study of Christian ethics.

Bill Moyers says, "When I'm asked to define Christian ethics, my best answer is Tom Maston. He showed us that the theater of Christian ethics is not the pulpit, the classroom or the counselor's corner, but all of life."

Now there is an antidote to secularism.

Churches and Taxation

Another application of Maston's church-state ethic involves the churches and taxation. He fears weakening or compromising the strong position of Baptists by their acceptance of tax exemptions. Through the years Maston has insisted that Baptists keep their noses clean by asking for no preferential treatment, by accepting no favors from government at any level, and by carrying their fair share of the civic load.

---

[41]Maston, *The Christian, the Church, and Contemporary Problems,* 196.

[42]Ibid., 197.

[43]Ibid., 198.

Specific proposals related to taxation of the churches include Maston's views that all church-owned "revenue-producing property should be taxed," that "we should not expect tax exemption on property owned by a church except that used for regular worship and educational purposes" and that "the housing allowance for church and denominational employees should not be tax-exempt."[44]

He goes beyond these generally accepted separationist views to suggest that "churches should voluntarily make a contribution for fire and police protection."[45]

Dr. Maston holds in creative tension his pleas for church-state separation and his warnings regarding an all-encompassing state, a totalitarian state with the power to deny religious freedom. In 1970, the United States Supreme Court ruled in favor of the traditional property tax exemptions for churches. *Walz v. Tax Commission*, 397 U.S. 664 (1970), held property tax exemptions for churches to be constitutional. Maston with Abner V. McCall, then president of Baylor University, myself, and others encouraged the Baptist General Convention of Texas to file a friend-of-the-court brief with the Supreme Court supporting the historic tax exemptions.

In his attitudes about the churches and taxes, as in many other regards, T. B. Maston holds progressive, creative, strong positions that trouble many of his peers. His stands are forceful and clear but balanced.

Civil Disobedience

Yet another timely implication of T. B. Maston's political ethic is his view of civil disobedience. Against the stream of popular opinion Maston doggedly holds his high view of the competency of the individual before God. His belief in soul freedom is behind, beneath, and above the understanding of specific roles of church or state. He appeals to the Acts account in which the followers of Jesus found it necessary to disobey the civil as well as the religious authorities.

Maston taught, however, that civil disobedience when appropriate should be engaged in regretfully and respectfully, with the disobedient fully prepared to accept the consequences. He was sympathetic with much of the civil disobedience of the civil rights movement and wrote, "each civil disobedience incident or movement would have to be judged on its own merits."[46]

---

[44]T. B. Maston, "Taxation Analyzed," *Baptist Standard* (28 May 1975): 19.
[45]Ibid.
[46]*The Conscience of a Christian*, 132.

Conscientious Objection

Closely related to Dr. Maston's perspective on civil disobedience is his support for conscientious objectors. During World War II, T. B. Maston believed that Southern Baptists should provide financial support for their own conscientious objectors to military service who were often interned in camps.

Maston has frequently pointed out through the years that the "peace churches" provided for the basic needs of many Southern Baptists whose consciences would not permit them to be a part of the war effort. Soul freedom stretches for Maston to allow a healthy acceptance of those with whom one disagrees. "Each Christian, regardless of his personal position concerning war, should defend and respect the right of conscience of every other Christian."[47]

CONCLUSION

The professor retains a vital interest in church-state issues. In 1984 and 1985 he warned in letters, conversations, and classrooms against the fundamentalist American Coalition for Traditional Values. The political agenda, the partisan identity, and the rightist philosophy of ACTV are all contrary to any belief in religious freedom. The leadership involvement of several presidents of the Southern Baptist Convention has seemed most bothersome to Dr. Maston.

The teacher of 10,000 Southern Baptist ethics students always has been opposed to government meddling in the churches, has been against idolatrous civil religion and ready to fight government-sponsored religious exercises in the public schools. He has seen the dangers in spending tax dollars for aid to private and parochial schools and, hence, has fought tuition tax credits and other forms of parochiaid. He has warned against an ambassador from the United States to the Roman Catholic Church or coziness with any religious group on the part of government.

Dr. Maston continues to stand behind and beside the denominational agency dedicated to protecting religious liberty and defending church-state separation. He supports the Baptist Joint Committee on Public Affairs in outspoken and effective ways.

True to his own teaching, T. B. Maston practices what he preaches. He validates and works out his Christian experience in the citizenship layers of life. One can be a good citizen and a good Christian.

In the last fifty years no one individual has affected Southern Baptists' attitudes toward government any more than T. B. Maston. He has done much

---

[47]Ibid., 138.

progressively to shape the political ethic and conservatively to retain the church-state separationist position. He has made an impact directly through his writing and indirectly through the many he taught. He has determined to some degree the way Southern Baptists deal with public policy both by his articulation of principles and his application of those principles to specific issues.

T. B. Maston has freely and imaginatively baptized, Southern style, the accommodation ethic and its nexus with theology, the realistic politics and other contributions of Reinhold Niebuhr. At the same time he has caught and passed along some of the passion for justice, the Christian sociology, and the lofty idealism of Walter Rauschenbush.

If the sprawling, squabbling Southern Baptist Convention has an identifiable political ethic other than a blurred reflection of the nation's mood at the moment, Maston has helped fashion it. If Southern Baptists make any sort of principled contribution to church-state questions it will be in large measure because T. B. Maston and his disciples have insisted on both active Christian citizenship and church-state separation.

THE HERMENEUTICS OF T. B. MASTON: REAPPRAISED AND EXTENDED

GUY GREENFIELD
SOUTHWESTERN BAPTIST SEMINARY
FT. WORTH TEXAS

INTRODUCTION

In early 1985 a student at Southwestern Seminary wrote to a former president of the Southern Baptist Convention. This well-known pastor had publicly charged that there were theological liberals in all six SBC seminaries. The student wrote to ask for documented evidence of who was liberal at Southwestern. He wrote, ''I am a student here, having taken several courses in Bible and theology, and am confused as to exactly which one of my professors is a liberal.''

The pastor responded by sending a document of several pages entitled ''Evidences,'' which included quotes from books and articles by several seminary professors and others. The document had no one's name on it as to compiler or source. The really interesting thing about it was that the only person referred to in the document who could be related to Southwestern was none other than Dr. T. B. Maston who retired in 1963, after a distinguished career of over forty years.

The Maston quote was unbelievable, to say the least. It came from a recent issue of *The Student* magazine (February 1985) from an article entitled,

"The Bible and Women," which Dr. Maston had published earlier in *Light,* a journal of the SBC Christian Life Commission. The quotation in "Evidences" was as follows:

> 1. Most of Paul's epistles were written to particular churches, in particular locations, faced with some particular problems.
> 2. This means that some portions of Paul's epistles are not directly relevant for our day; one example is the eating of meat offered to idols (Rom. 14; 1 Cor. 8-10).[1]

To call this "liberalism" is certainly stretching the meaning of the word if not a desperate attempt to discredit a retired Southwestern professor. This becomes more evident when Maston's third point is read from his article, a point carefully omitted in "Evidences."

> 3. Even in such passages, however, if we look deeply enough we will discover some basic principles that are relevant for every age.[2]

This quoting out of context is to be construed simply as another attempt on the part of some to discredit the faculty at Southwestern by trying to discredit one of the seminary's revered professors.

In his many years of teaching at Southwestern, Dr. Maston has at times been called "liberal" regarding his stand on certain social issues, particularly the race issue, but to my knowledge there is no reputably published and documented charge of liberalism that has been made regarding his stand on the Bible. If words mean anything at all, T. B. Maston has been as fundamental as any one regarding the nature and use of the Bible.

This essay on one level is an attempt to describe the hermeneutics of T. B. Maston. At another level, however, this essay is an effort to reappraise the way this renowned Christian ethicist interpreted the Bible for ethical decision making, for understanding the will of God regarding current social and moral issues, and for applying the Scriptures to modern-day life. I will also attempt, however, to present an extension of Maston's approach; that is, I have tried to go beyond Maston's principlism by the use of insights gained from value theory.

THE NATURE OF THE BIBLE

Maston's most recent statement on the Bible will be found in chapter one of *The Bible and Family Relations.* This was a revision of earlier material in *Why Live the Christian Life?* Before he launched into a study of the biblical

---

[1]Quoted in "Evidences" (mimeographed document) from T. B. Maston, *The Student* (February 1985): 47.

[2]T. B. Maston, *The Student* (February 1985): 47.

teachings on the family, Maston sought to establish the nature of his primary source.

Maston often perceived biblical truth through the method of tension-producing polarities. This is certainly the case in his use of "divine-human" to describe the nature of the Bible. It is not "either/or" but "both/and." The Bible was initiated by God but given through human mediation. Divine revelation on the stage of history was recorded by men inspired by the Spirit of God. Maston borrowed from Emil Brunner the suggestion that revelation is a "transitive event," that is, God is the subject of revelation while man is the object or recipient of revelation.

For Maston the Bible is the means through which God speaks today, but he would never equate the Bible with God since this would be idolatry. This is one primary reason Fundamentalists have never been happy with Maston. His position exposes their bibliolatry. Also, Maston never refers to the Bible as "inerrant," but then not one single Baptist confession of faith over the centuries does either. For Maston it is sufficient to consider the Bible authoritative, trustworthy, truthful, and dependable. "Inerrant" as a recent term has become a political catchword for control and manipulation. Such tactics Maston would consider as violations of the basic teachings of Scripture itself.

For Maston the Bible is not only divine-human in its composition but also in its substance. "It is a record of God's nature and character and of his attitude toward and will for humanity. But the Scriptures also portray the life struggles, the faults and failures, as well as the successes of real men and women."[3] Moreover, there is a unity of divine purpose in the midst of a diversity of human response throughout the Bible. This helps to explain many passages that seem contradictory to God's original purpose, for example, Moses' regulation of divorce (Deut. 24:1-4; Matt. 19:8-9).

Diversity also explains why the unity found in Scripture is dynamic rather than static. Such unity is one of growth and movement that is reminiscent of W. T. Conner's concept of "progressive revelation." This dynamic unity comes through most clearly from the divine Person revealed in Scripture seen through the central divine event: the birth, life, teachings, death, and resurrection of Jesus Christ, the climax of all biblical revelation. In Jesus we find the complete revelation of the nature and character of God, the Father, as well as God's attitude and desire for mankind.

Such revelation makes Christian faith primarily a religion of a Person rather than a religion of a Book. The Book is reverenced because of the Person recorded therein and not the reverse. This also means that the New Tes-

---

[3]T. B. Maston with William M. Tillman, Jr., *The Bible and Family Relations* (Nashville: Broadman Press, 1983) 18.

tament, particularly the life and teachings of Jesus, is normative for the people of God in all aspects of life. The Old Testament should always be read in light of the New. The Old Testament should never be granted equal authority with the New else one might end up expressing attitudes and behavior contrary to New Testament faith and practice.

Maston would never elevate the Old Testament over the life and teachings of Jesus because he believed so strongly in progressive revelation and because he held a very high view of Christology. Maston was noted for teaching that all the Bible is equally inspired but not all parts are equally valuable for faith and practice today. One does not go to Leviticus for an understanding of the resurrection nor to the Song of Songs for instructions on the Holy Spirit in the believer's life.

THE MESSAGE OF THE BIBLE

The teaching and writings of T. B. Maston set forth the Bible's essential message as twofold (note another tension-inducing polarity here): it tells people how to be saved and it tells saved people how to live. He would say that Fundamentalists tend to stress the former to the neglect of the latter while Liberals tend to stress the latter to the neglect of the former. Both overemphases are wrong. Heresy is always found at the extremes; orthodoxy stresses *balance*. Again, not either/or but both/and is needed in grasping the Bible's message.

The biblical message on how saved people ought to live involves two dimensions: (1) the vertical or being right with God, and (2) the horizontal or being right with other people as well as society at large. The vertical, obviously, is primary over the horizontal. The latter is derivative of the former, yet the latter is indicative of the validity of the former.

Maston was one of the few modern-day prophets who could see some of the theological and social inconsistencies among Southern Baptists who were good at preaching the gospel of personal salvation but so often were failures at living out this gospel in areas of human relationships (e.g., attitudes and behavior toward other races). For over fifty years this man has been calling Southern Baptists back to a balance of these two dimensions of biblical faith.

The biblical message is full of tension-inducing polarities that illustrate the two-dimensional nature of Christian faith: faith *and* works, worship *and* service, loving God *and* man, divine *and* human forgiveness, law *and* grace, cross *and* resurrection. With the contemporary resurgence of Fundamentalism, Southern Baptists today are in danger of losing touch with balance of the biblical message in its twofold dimension. For example, Maston would say today that Southern Baptists need *both* to hear the truth of God *and* learn to tell the truth to one another. The gospel is not only to be preached but also lived.

THE RELEVANCE OF THE BIBLE

Can an ancient book several centuries old have any relevance for us today? If that book is the Bible, T. B. Maston answers with a resounding "yes." Actually, if the Bible is studied carefully and interpreted properly, it will be found to be basically ahead rather than behind us and our times. Maston argues that modern man has yet to catch up with the ideals of the Bible.

This raises the question of culture. Certain biblical practices, such as the Levirate marriage law, the practice of betrothal, the custom of footwashing, the wearing of head coverings by women, the drinking of wine at meals and worship are not likely to be found in churches today. Yet the Bible discusses these matters. The question is, are these passages descriptive or prescriptive? Of course, it depends upon the presuppositions of the interpreter. How did Maston resolve this problem?

Dr. Maston began by suggesting that the abiding relevance of the Bible is found primarily in the Person revealed therein. God's self-disclosure gave birth to the Bible and this self-revelation is eternally relevant for people because they were created for fellowship with the Lord himself. Relevance is to be found in a relationship. Consequently, Maston's theology-ethics could be considered relational rather than merely conceptual. If the conceptual does not enhance the relational, there is something vitally missing in the conceptual.

Moreover, the redemptive message of Scripture is continuously relevant. People of all times and places need its message. Christianity is neither merely a first-century nor a twentieth-century faith. It is neither exclusively Palestinian nor American. It is a universal and inclusive faith seeking everyone whenever and wherever. Its truths transcend culture and calendar. Furthermore, the great promises of the Bible are eternally relevant speaking to all who will hear and claim them.

What about day-to-day decisions, problems, and relationships? What about the issues of the home, abortion, homosexuality, child abuse, working mothers, divorce, the single life versus marriage, sexual "freedom," alcoholism and drug abuse, living together outside of marriage, discipline of children, euthanasia, neglect of parents, and so forth? For Maston, the Bible is relevant for us in these and related modern-day problems if we read, study, and interpret the biblical text properly. However, "it is a *mistake* and will be disappointing *if we consider the Bible a rule book* to which we can turn for a chapter-and-verse answer to every question or a solution for every problem."[4]

The basic needs of humans remain relatively unchanged through the centuries, but specific needs or problems tend to vary from age to age and place to place. This was true in biblical times. Some of the biblical material is historically and culturally conditioned "written primarily to meet the needs of a particular group of people faced with some particular problems at a particular point in time."[5] Examples would be some of the ceremonial regulations in the Old Testament as well as some of Paul's instructions regarding eating meat offered to idols.

However, Maston argued that behind these regulations and instructions there lay ideals and principles that are abidingly relevant.[6] For example, in 1 Corinthians 8, 9, and 10 as well as in Romans 14 Paul's guiding principles regarding eating meat offered to idols are: (1) what is right for Christians is not decided totally by what they themselves consider to be the right thing to do; rather, what others consider right must be taken into account; (2) action that may be right within itself can become definitely wrong if it affects others harmfully; (3) love must be the determinative factor rather than knowledge since knowledge may produce arrogance while love always strengthens relationships.

Moreover, more important to Maston than the words of Scripture were the actions, attitudes, and spirit of the biblical characters. This would be particularly true with regard to Jesus in the Gospels that set forth not only his teachings but also the quality of life he lived. He lived everything he taught. Therefore, the careful interpreter of Scripture must seek to "*capture its spirit, which may be as relevant and possibly more so than its words.*"[7] Again, it is obvious why Maston has not been popular among the wooden literalists of Fundamentalism, but then, neither was his colleague W. T. Conner.

A METHOD OF INTERPRETING THE BIBLE:
A PRINCIPLIST APPROACH

For T. B. Maston the Bible has always been clear and powerful in and of itself. To read and meditate upon the text of Scripture has been the pattern of

---

[4]Ibid., 25.

[5]Ibid., 26.

[6]James Giles, "Biblical Ethics," in *An Approach to Christian Ethics: The Life, Contribution, and Thought of T. B. Maston,* compiled by William M. Pinson, Jr. (Nashville: Broadman Press, 1979) 99-110.

[7]Maston, *The Bible and Family Relations,* 26-27.

his life and ministry. However, such a conviction in no way depreciates the need for sound principles of interpretation. Even in the Bible there are examples of the need to interpret the text, for example, Philip and the eunuch (Acts 8:26-40), and Jesus' interpreting Scripture to the two disciples on the road to Emmaus (Luke 24:27).

Maston's hermeneutics operated around three objectives that he learned from H. E. Dana, a former colleague at Southwestern. First, the interpreter must reach the historical objective: what did the text mean to the first readers? Second, the universal objective must be gained, that is, what is the overarching universal principle grounded in the historical context that is not bound by time and place? Third, the practical objective becomes the controlling interest of the interpreter, that is, how does the universal principle apply to concrete situations here and now? In other words, orthodoxy in truth must lead to orthopraxy in life.

In addition, the interpreter needs to approach Scripture with certain proper attitudes that are shaped and formed by several guidelines. Maston's working hermeneutical presuppositions are as follows:

1. A reverence for God and a deep desire to know and do his will.

2. Belief in the inspiration and authority of the Scriptures.

3. Reverently read and study the Bible.

4. Approach the study with a searching mind, not looking for proof texts to support a preconceived position but honestly searching for the truth.

5. Realize that the Bible represents a progressive revelation becoming more clear as it nears completion.

6. Understand that any translation, such as our Bibles, inevitably involves some interpretation.

7. Recognize that many portions of the Scriptures have to be interpreted.

8. Welcome the work of biblical scholars who help get us closer to the original words and meaning of the Scriptures.

9. Critically use the interpretation of others, such as carefully and reverently written commentaries.

10. Understand, however, that we as individual Christians have the right and the accompanying responsibility to read and interpret the Scriptures for ourselves.[8]

Moreover, interpreting the Bible calls for hermeneutical principles. Maston has sought to follow these:

1. Relate as far as possible any particular Scripture to its background and its historical situation.

2. Give proper consideration to the context.

---

[8]Ibid., 28.

3. Use Scripture to interpret Scripture. Utilize clear teachings to clarify the less clear.

4. Recognize that usually the most natural interpretation of a particular Scripture is more likely to be correct than a more involved interpretation.

5. Christian experience is not a substitute for a knowledge of the Bible, but it can be a valuable factor in the correct interpretation of the Scriptures. If our interpretation . . . conflicts with our experiences as Christians, we may need to reexamine our interpretation or reinterpret our experiences.

6. In some biblical statements, the spirit of the statement should be our guide rather than its specific words. Commands or teachings in terms of one culture must be translated into our culture.

7. A distinction should be made between what the Bible records and what it approves.

8. Commands to individuals in biblical days are not necessarily the will of God for us.

9. Acknowledge the need for and seek the guidance of the Holy Spirit as we interpret the Scriptures.

10. While it may not properly be called a principle, a sincere desire to live in harmony with the truth discovered in the Bible is an important factor in understanding what our Father would say to us in and through the Scriptures.[9]

Once the text has been exegeted, however, how does the interpreter bring the then and there to the here and now? Only in scattered and limited statements does Maston give any explanation of his method. Basically, one has to examine his writings to see his method in action.

For Maston, the principlist approach is one of identifying the abiding principles of Scripture and applying those principles to life today. The nearest Maston ever comes to a clear definition of "principle" is his use of certain concepts as possible synonyms, such as *ideals,* or more specifically, *ideals of perfection.*[10]

Probably, Maston's treatment of the nature of the Christian life reflects the primary principles or ideals to be derived from Scripture: (1) Its highest motive, the glory of God; (2) Its ultimate authority, the will of God; (3) Its supreme value, the kingdom of God; (4) Its comprehensive ideal, perfection; (5) Its crowning virtue, love; (6) Its unifying symbol, the cross; (7) Its continuing problem, tension.[11]

The last concept, tension, is a primary Mastonian idea. Fond of quoting Reinhold Niebuhr's term for these ideals as "impossible possibilities," Mas-

[9]Ibid., 29-30.

[10]T. B. Maston, *Why Live the Christian Life?* (Nashville: Broadman Press, 1974) 59.

[11]Ibid., vi-vii.

ton held that the biblical ideals serve as a constant challenge to and judgment upon every human imperfect approximation. "They are above and beyond history, eternally transcendent but also, and for that reason, eternally relevant. These ideals of perfection create the dynamic tension at the heart of our Christian faith, which, in turn, is the secret to its creativity."[12]

For Maston, such concepts as the kingdom of God, love, and the cross are not necessarily the same as the general principles he derives from Scripture that provide more concrete guidance for ethical decision making (such as justice, impartiality, or respect for others). Rather, these principles approximate more closely what might be called themes or motifs that when applied to the context of a biblical text serve as regulatory values to explain the relevant character and intent of the passage. These same concepts or themes nevertheless stand as exemplary ideals toward which the Christian is to strive in all aspects of his or her life. Therefore, they perform a dual function, both as motifs or themes of interpretation and as standards for living.

The term "principle" for Maston basically then refers to a *concept* that reflects an ideal that flows out of the revealed will of God. These ideals, which are inherent in the biblical principles, provide tone and direction for Christian living. "They will not only help us to know the will of God, they also will deepen our desire to walk in his will. They will even provide a basis for the proper interpretation of the specific teachings of the Bible."[13]

Examples of such concepts are holiness, righteousness, love, justice, mercy, impartiality, and self-denial. These and other similar principles of a general nature are especially prominent in the life and teachings of Jesus. Actually, Jesus "restricted himself in his teachings, in the main, to the enunciation of general principles or ideals. That is one reason for the abiding relevance of his teachings."[14]

Therefore, understanding the nature of these revealed principles renders all of Scripture contemporary. By their very character, they reveal the nature of God and his will. Although the Bible sets forth specific laws, rules, regulations, directives, and instructions, many of which are historically conditioned, "it may be that behind the particular prescription or law there lies some principle or principles that are continually relevant and, hence, abidingly valid and authoritative. To use Piper's term, there is at least, revealed in the Scriptures 'a view of life' that is relevant and authoritative."[15]

---

[12]Ibid., 59.

[13]T. B. Maston, *God's Will and Your Life* (Nashville: Broadman Press, 1964) 65.

[14]Ibid.

[15]T. B. Maston, *Biblical Ethics* (Macon GA: Mercer University Press, 1967) xiv.

For Maston, some of Paul's specific statements are largely, if not entirely, irrelevant for us today, such as those regarding women speaking in church and the eating of certain meats. "However, if we examine carefully enough we shall discover even in what seems to be the most irrelevant portions of his epistles deep-seated principles that governed the life of Paul and principles that are abidingly relevant for the child of God."[16]

Yet, only partially and in limited fashion did Maston set forth any systematic treatment of the principles to be derived from carefully exegeted passages. Even in his *Biblical Ethics* Maston was primarily describing what the Bible says on ethical themes. Also, he wrote more as a biblical theologian than as a biblical ethicist-exegete. He did not teach us *how* to take a passage and derive the relevant principles for today. Again, he dealt more with a description of the then and there of the text than with the *methodology* for discovering the here and now application.

Nowhere have I found a Mastonian *methodology* for differentiating between the culturally relative and the abidingly relevant. He will often identify the difference but not explain how he differentiated. I once put this same problem before Carl F. H. Henry when he was a guest in one of the Ph.D. seminars I was teaching. His response was that he had not developed a satisfactory methodology either. It is interesting that the following year Henry sat on the resolutions committee of the 1984 Southern Baptist Convention that presented a resolution on women in ministry (Henry read it before the SBC session that voted on it). It is interesting that this resolution based its negative view of women only on Paul's and Peter's statements without any reference to a word from Jesus.

There has not been much written on methodology with regard to deriving principles from the biblical texts. Two recent works have been extremely helpful in this area of research: Allen Verhey's *The Great Reversal: Ethics and the New Testament* (Eerdmans, 1984) and Richard Longenecker's *New Testament Social Ethics for Today* (Eerdmans, 1984). It is hoped such works will encourage writers of future commentaries to engage in differentiating between the culturally relative and the abidingly relevant.

AN EXTENSION OF PRINCIPLISM

Some Christian ethicists who work with the biblical materials would criticize Maston's principlism as little different from legalism, methodologically speaking. That is to say, a principle functions essentially the same as a stated law or regulation. I would agree if one bases one's methodology strictly on

[16]Ibid, 179.

a rationalistic approach. However, Maston's hermeneutics go beyond rationalism to include a strong emphasis on one's relationship with the central Person in the Bible: God revealed in Jesus Christ.

Such a relational hermeneutic stresses not only the need to understand the background, words, and intention of the text but also to depend heavily on such considerations as the illuminating guidance of the Holy Spirit, prayer, the insights of a community of faith as well as the insights from church history, a willingness to trust and obey God, an informed conscience, as well as the use of sound judgement based upon the interactions of the data of the situation at hand with others, self, and God.[17]

In my own efforts to work with the biblical texts for contemporary decision making, I have tried to go beyond Maston to make some attempt at developing a hermeneutical methodology. I am clearly building upon Maston's approach, so I call it "an extension."

Value Theory and Hermeneutics

Values are similar to what Maston calls ideals. However, ideals reflect too much of an "out-of-reach" perfection. In my judgment, perfection is more of a Greek idea than a biblical one. For example, Matthew 5:48 has been grossly misunderstood. "Be ye perfect" should be translated "Be ye mature." The word translated perfect (*teleios*) is a relational term (the context is the unconditional love of God) suggesting process, growth, movement toward integrity and mercy (see Luke 6:36) and not a static term suggesting an impossible and unattainable goal that would merely frustrate human effort to reach it. The Greek idea also contributes to making perfectionistic and unloving people who in turn express conditional love toward others.

Values may be defined culturally as the ideals, customs, institutions, and concepts of a society toward which the people have an affective regard. Such values may be either positive or negative, that is, to be sought or avoided (e.g., peace or war). A value may be any object or quality desirable as a means or as an end in itself. Value and worth imply intrinsic excellence or desirability. Value is that quality of anything that renders it desirable or useful. Worth implies especially spiritual qualities of mind and character, or moral excellence, for example, "Few knew her true worth." Values may also be seen as goals we pursue in life.

It seems to me that principles, therefore, should be defined not as concepts but as *statements of value*. These are those general statements or guidelines, expressions of value, or guides to thinking and action that enter into moral discourse and activity. Many will be reminded here of John Bennett's "middle axioms." While rules are concrete and give direction to action in

---

[17]Maston, *God's Will,* Part II.

definite ways, principles are more abstract and offer guidelines rather than directions.

Consequently, I would define biblical principles as statements of value based upon some aspect of biblical revelation that provide guidelines for decision and/or action that are in harmony with the character of God revealed in Jesus Christ. A more complex classification of biblical principles has been developed by Harold DeWolf in his *Responsible Freedom,* chapter seven.[18] From a different perspective, Philip Wogaman derived from the biblical material what he calls ''presumptions'' in his *A Christian Method of Moral Judgment.*[19]

Value Classification

There are various ways of classifying values. Four seem to be primary in biblical ethics. First are *cultural values:* those values that reflect the ethos of the culture of a society that are to be achieved, expressed, and internalized by the individual and community. Examples are cleanliness, faithfulness, health, work, or learning.

Second are *social values:* those values that enhance and make for harmony in one's social relationships, that contribute to the integration, stability, and functioning of the society, and that are to be internalized and expressed by the individual and community in all relationships. Examples are law, marriage, honesty, fairness, truthfulness, or life.

Third are *spiritual values:* those values that provide meaning, purpose, direction, and a degree of eternal transcendence, and a degree of social unity for the members of the society, that are rooted in the religious and philosophical belief systems of the people, and that are to be internalized and expressed by the individual and community in all relationships. Examples are God, life, justice, faith, hope, love, family, freedom, service, worship, religious symbols, and so forth.

Fourth are *moral values:* those values that reflect a sense of oughtness in all relationships involving decisions of right and wrong, that are rooted in the religious and philosophical belief systems of the people, and that are to be internalized and expressed by the people individually and socially. Examples are honesty, justice, truth, marital fidelity, sexual propriety, racial harmony, freedom, and trustworthiness. At some points these values may tend to overlap. Certain values may fall into more than one category, for example, justice

---

[18]L. Harold DeWolf, *Responsible Freedom: Guidelines for Christian Action* (New York: Harper and Row, 1971).

[19]J. Philip Wogaman, *A Christian Method of Moral Judgment* (Philadelphia: Westminster, 1976).

is a spiritual, social, and a moral value. In some cultures it is a cultural value. This typology simply differentiates the variety of values in a society.

Also, in most societies and over time, values are in flux to some degree. American society has undergone considerable change in values during the twentieth century alone. See Daniel Yankelovich's *New Rules* (Random House, 1981) for an excellent treatment of such change. In biblical times an emphasis on the value of the tribe or nation tended to shift to the individual.

Within each category of values, there tends to be a *hierarchy* of values where some values are more important, of greater value, than others when such values come into conflict with each other in certain situations. For example, human life is usually of greater value than truth-telling; marriage is of greater value than friendship; or justice is of greater value than security.

Hermeneutical Levels

Concerning the role of values and principles in the interpretation of biblical texts, I have developed four levels of hermeneutics in the following order:

1. The directive, command, law, regulation, or instruction of the biblical text itself. Example: "Thou shalt not kill."

2. The value undergirding the text. Example: human life.

3. The principle or statement of the value. Example: human life is sacred and should be preserved, cared for, enhanced, and lived out for the glory of God its Creator.

4. The application of the principle. An example: human life should not be arbitrarily destroyed by abortion except in rare justifiable cases such as to save the life of the mother, where one value prevails over another.

These levels can be applied to any passages of Scripture that contain directives, commands, laws, regulations, instructions, or advice calling for some kind of human response or decision. Even Paul's instructions regarding women or his advice to Timothy about drinking wine for his stomach trouble can be applied to today with this method. The values of the gospel in orderly worship and the physical health of the body can be applied to today without making Paul look ridiculous in contemporary culture.

Values and Biblical Ethics

Values are the basis for biblical ethics. It was Richard Niebuhr who said that faith is the "attitude and action of confidence in, and fidelity to, certain realities as the sources of value and the objects of loyalty. . . . it involves reference to the value that attaches to the self and to the value toward which the self is directed. On the one hand it is trust in that which gives value to the self; on the other hand it is loyalty to what the self values.''[20] The Bible reflects clusters of values that were expressed over many centuries by God's covenant people, especially the biblical writers as they were inspired by God.

Moreover, the values reflected in the Bible may be classified by the above typology: cultural, social, spiritual, and moral. Also, the rules, commandments, regulations, advice, and instructions recorded in Scripture were based upon these values.

In addition, sound hermeneutics require that the contemporary interpreter distinguish between not only the types of values but also between the permanent and the passing character of their revelational validity as reflected in the biblical statements. This calls for distinguishing between the abidingly relevant and the culturally relative. Identifying the biblical value behind the text will aid in this decision.

Behind every biblical command, regulation, directive, instruction, and teaching stands a value that may be expressed in statement form called a *principle*. The permanent aspect of a biblical teaching reflects a value (cultural, social, spiritual, or moral) that is of eternal and universal validity because it reflects some element of the character and will of God. The passing aspect of a biblical teaching reflects a value that was rooted in a specific historical time-place situation that has been corrected or modified by either subsequent revelation or the generally accepted practice of the people of God, for example, from Sabbath to the Lord's Day for worship.

Biblical teachings need to be translated into permanent principles for relevant contemporary application. Principles are derived by identifying the values reflected in the biblical material and discerning which of these values reflect the character and will of God. The full range of biblical revelation must serve as the total context for such discernment utilizing the hermeneutical perspective of progressive revelation and recognizing that the Bible has a built-in corrective process that the Holy Spirit used to provide us with the final revelation of God's truth in Jesus Christ. This corrective process was not a correction of early false teaching by later true teaching but a correction of early partial, incomplete, or dim truth by later full, complete, and clear truth.

Biblical principles, therefore, serve as guidelines for contemporary ethical decision making for which the individual Christian must assume responsibility yet in dialogue with Scripture, in dependence upon the illumination of the Holy Spirit, and in the context of the fellowship, support, and shared insights of a community of faith (a local church), as well as the larger community of Christian history. This approach is very close to and compatible

---

[20]H. Richard Niebuhr, *Radical Monotheism and Western Culture* (New York: Harper Torchbooks, 1960) 16.

with the "response style" of decision making recommended by Everding and Wilbanks (*Decision Making and the Bible,* Judson Press, 1975).

CONCLUSION

Thanks to the hermeneutics of T. B. Maston, contemporary biblical interpreters can continue to hold to a very high view of the Bible as the Word of God and to find meaningful relevance of its teachings for any age and any place without surrendering to the rigid woodenness of Fundamentalism and its often ridiculous conclusions regarding what the Bible teaches for today. As Maston himself once wrote, "The Bible is the most important possession of the Christian churches, far more important than all of their buildings, institutions, and endowments. Protestants who give to it a 'unique and unrivaled place of authority' need in a special way to be acquainted with it and to see the relevance of its basic concepts and principles to the life of the individual and the world in which he lives."[21]

---

[21]Maston, *Biblical Ethics,* xi.

MAJOR LIFE SHAPERS: MARRIAGE AND THE FAMILY

JULIAN C. BRIDGES
HARDIN-SIMMONS UNIVERSITY
ABILENE TEXAS

INTRODUCTION

Every author brings his or her background to what is written. The present writer is no exception. Therefore, what follows is a composite of the contributions of many men and women to the writer's life. With regard to the topic at hand, however, clearly two scholars stand out in bold relief—T. B. Maston and Gerald R. Leslie.[1]

Dr. Maston was my first major instructor on marriage and the family, although I also obtained some exposure to the topic as a university undergraduate. After arriving at the seminary, every course available on the family was taken—most of them under Maston—and the doctoral dissertation was also

---

[1]Gerald R. Leslie is a very well-known scholar in the field of family sociology. He has been President of the National Council on Family Relations and of the American Association of Marriage Counselors (now Marriage and Family Therapists) and is the author of widely used textbooks in sociology. He chaired the Department of Sociology at the University of Florida when the present writer obtained his M.A. and Ph.D. in sociology and taught all seminars that were taken in the area of the family. Leslie's text, *The Family in Social Context,* is now in an unprecedented sixth edition (currently coauthored with Korman) and is drawn on heavily for the social science content included in this chapter.

written, largely under Maston's direction, on a topic related directly to family life.[2]

What impressed me almost immediately was not only the excellence of Maston's teaching and its direct applicability, but that his approach was not limited to theological literature. He explored religious research in depth, but he was not willing to stop there. Rather, he delved into the social and behavioral sciences particularly, in order to permit his students to be abreast of the latest research findings on the family in these fields also. Since I had behavioral science as one of my undergraduate majors at a large public institution, it was very gratifying to find a professor such as T. B. Maston who had integrated the contributions of nonreligious research on the family with religious investigations in order to provide the greatest orientation and insight into the nature of family life. It is my view also that the theological and the socioscientific can complement each other and offer a much more complete picture of how to help solve the numerous problems that often challenge the stability of families in the modern world.

Obviously, space here does not permit an adequate treatment of Maston's total family ethic. His latest, most comprehensive statement on this subject is found in a recent book, *The Bible and Family Relations.*[3] Therefore, I have chosen to focus first on Maston's emphasis on the importance of the family and then on a few aspects of family life that are of immediate interest and relevancy today because of the changes that are occurring in these areas of family relations.

IMPORTANCE OF THE FAMILY

Maston has stressed the importance of the family indirectly by simply choosing to speak and write more frequently in this area. In a letter to author John C. Howell, Maston personally penned the following: "I have done more writing and speaking about the family than anything else."[4]

Nevertheless, Maston is very clear in his writing on family topics to state directly just how important he feels the family is. In fact, I have found no other theologian who is as emphatic about the preeminence of the family among all the major social institutions—government, economic life, educa-

---

[2]Since the author was preparing for a career in foreign mission service, the topic chosen was "An Examination of Some Aspects of Family Morality in Latin America," unpublished Th.D. dissertation, Southwestern Baptist Theological Seminary, 1961.

[3]T. B. Maston and William M. Tillman, Jr., *The Bible and Family Relations* (Nashville: Broadman Press, 1983).

[4]John C. Howell, "Marriage and Family," in *An Approach to Christian Ethics,* compiled by William M. Pinson, Jr. (Nashville: Broadman Press, 1979) 120.

tion, and religion—as is Maston. He states it succinctly when he says: "The home is God's first institution: first in time and first in importance."[5] A few sentences later he elaborates:

> It is a more important educational institution than the school, a more important institution for law and order than the state, and even a more basically important religious institution than the church. There is no surer barometer of the condition of a culture than the health or sickness of its families. As the home goes, so goes everything else: school, church, and civilization itself.[6]

With regard to why the home is more significant than even the church, Maston reasons: "Really about all the churches can do is try to supplement what the home has done or to make up for what it has not done. And the church cannot completely make up for the failure of the home."[7] Parents are the principal educators of their children. Principles taught or not taught in the home will determine whether individuals become citizens who obey the laws of society or not. The family likewise, more than any other one institution, influences whether its members live out on a daily basis the teachings of the church presented only one or two days a week.

In conjunction with this strong emphasis on the value of the family vis-a-vis the other social institutions, it is interesting to note the observations of some leading social scientists on the same subject. Margaret Mead, probably the most reputable American anthropologist of this century, says that the family is the "toughest institution we have. It is, in fact, the institution to which we owe our humanity."[8] Leslie and Korman, noted family sociologists, state that the family is the basic social institution. It is universal and particularly so in that it "is always a conspicuous feature of social organization" in any society from the most simple tribe to the most complex, highly urbanized nation.[9] Still another scientist states:

> The idea of the family is a reference point for people. A family represents love, security, and certain values even if, in reality, one's own family is mean-minded and distant. Families . . . connote responsibility, especially

---

[5]Maston and Tillman, *The Bible and Family,* 56.

[6]Ibid., 57.

[7]T. B. Maston, "The Bible and Family Relations," Family Life Tapes (Fort Worth: Latimer House, 1976), cited by Howell, 122.

[8]Margaret Mead, "The Impact of Cultural Changes on the Family," *The Family in the Urban Community* (Detroit: The Merrill-Palmer School, 1953) 4, cited by Gerald R. Leslie and Sheila K. Korman, *The Family in Social Context,* 6th ed. (New York: Oxford University Press, 1985) 3.

[9]Leslie and Korman, *The Family,* 11-12.

toward the very young and very old. People believe that families are the group of first and last resort.[10]

Social scientists also point out that the family alone, among all the social institutions, fulfills at least partially all of the requisites for a society's survival: the sexual, reproductive, residential, economic functions, and the socialization of the young for maintaining order (the political) and developing values concerning the meaning of life and the motivation for group and individual survival (the religious).[11]

Another distinctive emphasis concerning the importance of the family that Maston makes is that God has written in human nature the ideal laws with respect to marriage and the family. These laws are set out in the Bible. In other words, biblical teaching is the ideal not just for believers but also for nonbelievers of the Christian faith. Maston affirms: "God does not have one set of basic laws for the Christian couple and another set for the non-Christian."[12]

Such a statement, of course, is not within the purview of social science to discuss. Nevertheless, it is worth noting that social scientists often spend considerable time and energy researching problems that develop within societies and cultures when they deviate from the biblical ideals.

THE ROLE OF WOMEN

As is true for all of Maston's writing, he builds a basis for his conclusions on biblical teaching. After a thorough analysis of passages throughout the Bible that deal with women's roles, he draws a number of conclusions. A few of them are quoted here:

> The clearest statement of God's plan and will for women in the Old Testament is found in the creation accounts (Gen. 1 and 2). The major emphases are that woman, as well as man, was created in the image of God; that either is incomplete without the other; and that they are to be partners that supplement or complement each other. The latter is not just true in the marriage state but in their relationship in general.

> The final and complete revelation of God, including his will for men and women, is found in the life and teachings of Jesus. He was deeply concerned about people, particularly the neglected and underprivileged, including women and children.

---

[10]Robert W. Fogel, et al., eds., *Aging: Stability and Change in the Family* (New York: Academic Press, 1981) xix, cited by Leslie and Korman, 13.

[11]Leslie and Korman, *The Family,* 17.

[12]Maston and Tillman, *The Bible and Family,* 43.

The only clear restriction concerning women by Jesus was the fact that he did not include any of them in the twelve. That doubtlessly would have created some serious problems for him and for his whole ministry in the culture in which he operated.

Paul, who has been grossly misinterpreted if not maligned regarding some things he said concerning women, needs to be restudied in the light of his relation to women and the nature of his ministry, as well as some specific things he said concerning women.[13]

Regarding woman's creation, as referred to in Genesis 1:26-31, Maston quotes Old Testament scholar Heflin as follows: "Woman in this passage is certainly no inferior afterthought; she is rather one with man in the responsibility of subduing the creation and propagating the race."[14] Maston makes a great deal of two biblical facts: that both man and woman are created equally in God's image (Gen. 1:27) and that Jesus Christ died to restore that image, marred but not totally destroyed by sin. These two facts, Maston says, "should be the basis for our respect for persons, regardless of sex, race, culture, or condition of life. This means, among other things, that no person, male or female, should ever be used as a mere means. Each person is an end of infinite value."[15]

Maston deals with Genesis 3:16, which is often used by those who seek to justify making women subservient to men, in the following manner:

> Following the temptation and fall, it is said that the man or husband was to rule over the woman or his wife. Through the centuries and even today there is some difference of opinion whether the statement was and is to be considered prescriptive or descriptive. G. Ernest Wright says that "the equality of the sexes is within the order of creation . . . the subservience of woman to man belongs to the 'fallen world.' " He further says that the verses of judgment in Genesis 3, including verse 16, "are simply descriptions of the way things are in the world as it is." The actual situation concerning the family in the Old Testament fell far below God's original plan and purpose for marriage and the home: polygamy, concubinage, divorce, and so forth.[16]

Thus, Maston maintains and insists that the Bible teaches the equality of men and women, even though there are obvious differences between the two sexes. These differences contribute toward enriching the personhood of each. Since God has personhood, those created in his image likewise have the ability to think, feel, choose, and communicate. "Persons," Maston states, "are

[13]Ibid., 81.

[14]Quoted in Maston and Tillman, *The Bible and Family,* 65.

[15]Ibid.

[16]Ibid., 55.

not only capable of communication, but communication with other persons is necessary. There is no person without other persons.''[17] As far as we know, man did not speak until woman was created. Man was not completely a person without woman to complement him. The two need each other and are created as equals.

Maston makes the following statement as it relates to the matter of authority in male-female relationships:

> In Christ the image of God is equally restored in both men and women through their union with him. The only person who has the right or authority to rule over woman is the Ruler of the universe, who has the right to rule over men as well as women. But even the Lord does not force his authority on anyone. It must be voluntarily accepted; when accepted, we will discover that his yoke is easy and his burden is light (Matt. 11:30). In other words, his rule and authority is best for us. This is true in our individual lives and in our relationships as men and women, husbands and wives, parents and children.[18]

Social scientists indicate that of the six general components of the worldwide change toward some form of conjugal or nuclear family, three of these trends involve greater rights for women: free choice of spouse for both sexes, equal status for women, and equal rights for divorce.[19] It is doubtful that these trends will reverse themselves, since they seem to be causally related to factors such as urbanization, industrialization, the rise of individualism, the desire for economic progress, and the growth of equalitarianism. These patterns are becoming increasingly popular throughout the developing as well as the developed countries of the world.

In the United States an increasing number and proportion of women work outside the home each year. A number of studies have demonstrated that wives' decision-making power increases as they move outside the home into the labor market.[20] In all age categories beyond age seventeen, a majority of women are now working. Wives' participation in the labor force varies with age, education, income, and the presence or absence and number of children. However, now not only a majority of mothers with children under age 18 work away from home but a majority of those with children under age six are now in that category also. A decline in the birth rate and an increase in the divorce rate in recent years have contributed greatly to this trend.

---

[17]Ibid., 64-65.

[18]Ibid., 68.

[19]Leslie and Korman, *The Family,* 75.

[20]Francine D. Blau, ''Women in the Labor Force: An Overview,'' in *Women: A Feminist Perspective,* 3rd ed. (Palo Alto CA: Mayfield Publishing Company, 1984) 302-303.

All social scientists with whom the author is familiar predict that the proportion of women working will continue to increase until women will comprise over one-half of the total labor force in the United States in the near future. In some age categories, as high as ninety percent of all women eligible to work will do so. This should contribute to further equality for women in American society.

With the movement toward equality so evident in social institutions such as economic life, politics, and education, what of women's roles and status in the institution of religion? In a section entitled "Application" within his chapter on "Women," Maston arrives at the heart of the issue concerning the role of women in the contemporary church in America. A few of his more salient points are:

> Many churches and church leaders need to reconsider the attitude of the churches toward women and the place they give them in their program and work.
>
> Women should be given more of a voice in the programs and structures of many of our churches.
>
> Some churches, pastors, and other church leaders may be hesitant about doing anything about giving women more of a voice because of a fear that it will disturb the peace of the church and church family.
>
> Such hesitation may in some cases be justified. However, it should not be defended as God's ultimate will concerning women in our churches. In many, and possibly most, of our churches, women are not treated as Jesus would treat them or as our Father would have them treated.[21]

Maston then tackles the touchy topic of the ordination of women. He believes that the entire matter of New Testament ordination needs to be restudied. Biblical ordination was probably a very simple service, compared to what some churches have now made it. If there is a return to the biblical example, then "the only concern of a church should be whether God had called the individual to some phase of specialized ministry. The so-called 'ordination service' would be primarily a dedication service."[22] Maston also feels that ordination should not be sought by either men or women but should emerge as a request from others, unless it is actually needed to perform some specific task. Maston has questioned through the years if ordination was actually necessary in many cases, and he often reminded his readers and his ministerial students that he himself has never been ordained to the preaching ministry.

---

[21]Maston and Tillman, *The Bible and Family,* 82.

[22]Ibid., 82-83.

Perhaps it is worth noting that at the time of this writing, less than one percent of all ordained ministers in the Southern Baptist Convention are female. Nevertheless, the number has grown phenomenally in recent years. A publication dated 1976 states that there were only ''about 15 ordained women,'' whereas the number presently is estimated to be about 350, and more than 100 of these were ordained in the previous twelve months.[23]

Without encouraging the ordination of women as either deacons, deaconesses, or ministers, Maston does not directly oppose it. He quotes the highly respected Southern Baptist scholar A. T. Robertson with respect to the woman mentioned in Romans 16:1: ''in some sense Phoebe was a servant [deacon] or minister of the church in Cenchreae.''[24]

Typical of his ability to bring balance to controversial issues, Maston's concluding statement to the entire chapter on women is:

> In this whole awakening of interest in women and their place in the home, the church, and society, it will be tragic if we ever belittle the traditional role of the woman as wife and mother. Even in the contemporary world with all the freedom that women have, this role should be given priority.[25]

HUSBAND AND WIFE RELATIONSHIPS

Maston begins his chapter on husbands and wives with the reminder that so goes a marriage, so goes the family in general, and ultimately, so goes a society and civilization. If, indeed, a marriage is of such strategic importance, is it not possible that one of the greatest shortcomings and sins committed today is that as spouses and other family members we tend to take each other for granted? Are the courteous expressions, ''please'' and ''thank you,'' too often omitted in conversations at home? Is the same patience and understanding exercised in listening to the problems of a work associate not in short supply when a family member has a need? Are physical checkups necessary for good individual health but marriage checkups totally out of order? Are goals for improving the house or one's job acceptable, without ever setting goals for growing a better marriage? When our home becomes a high priority, beginning with our marriage or family, then it begins to move toward re-

---

[23]Priscilla Proctor and William Proctor, *Women in the Pulpit* (Garden City: Doubleday and Co., Inc., 1976) 21, cited by Marguerite Woodruff, ''Women in Church and Society,'' in Pinson, 138; and ''Women in the Church,'' *Abilene Reporter-News,* 15 June 1985, 7C.

[24]Maston and Tillman, *The Bible and Family,* 84.

[25]Ibid., 83.

alizing its maximum potential, and concomitantly its effect on the lives of individual family members begins to bear unbelievably beautiful fruit.

Maston stresses time and again the importance and the sacredness of the marriage relationship. He discusses in detail the choice of a life companion and says that it is comparable to deciding on a life career. The only choice of greater significance in one's entire life is how one chooses to relate to Jesus Christ. Therefore, selecting a marriage partner should be permeated by prayer, not only by the individuals directly involved but by their parents as well. Every marriage of a Christian ought only to be with another Christian, and preferably with one of the same denomination.

Maston states that "God's original and his continuing purpose for marriage was and is one man and one woman joined together as husband and wife for life."[26] He then embarks on a discussion of what he terms "Contrasting Perspectives" in the Bible, regarding the qualities of and relationships between husbands and wives.

One of the principal contrasts is the importance of always maintaining a balance between the ideal and the real. According to Maston, the Apostle Paul had this challenge. He said that among those who have faith in Christ, "there is neither male nor female" (Gal. 3:28). Yet in another passage (Eph. 5:22-24), Paul suggests that wives should be subject or submissive to their husbands. Maston feels that Paul was saying that men and women were called to freedom in Christ—a radical ideal for his day—but they were not to use that freedom in an unbridled manner. Rather, he counseled, "through love be servants of one another" (Gal. 5:13).

Maston explains Paul's contrasting perspective with these words:

> It seems that Paul was fearful that some of the new converts, particularly wives and slaves, would go too far too fast in exercising the new freedom they had in Christ. This explains his conservative application of the radical idea.[27]

Maston then applies this principle to the needs of modern pastors and other church leaders to always proclaim the ideal but apply it according to where their congregation is and lead them from there toward attaining the ideal. The result of this practice is to continually create a healthy tension, which is always "abidingly relevant." Without tension there is little, if any, progress toward ever reaching the ideal.

As a contemporary example of contrasting perspectives, Maston discusses the hierarchical or "chain-of-command" model of marriage and family life as compared to the democratic or "partnership" model. He soundly

---

[26]Ibid., 162

[27]Ibid., 163

rejects the former as being based upon Bible verses taken out of context and inconsistently interpreted. Agreeing with Jewett, he quotes him as stating: "man and woman are properly related when they accept each other as equals whose differences are mutually complementary in all spheres of life and human endeavour."[28]

Maston again makes reference to the concept of the image of God, as it applies also to husband-wife relations. This concept means that men and women in marriage both stand in the presence of God as equals. "This equality is deepened and made more meaningful when they are brought into union with Christ. In him there is no male or female (Gal. 3:28)."[29] This means that they should each be treated with respect, should never be used or manipulated, and should always be treated as a "thou" [person] and never as an "it" [object].

Although men and women are equals, they are still created male and female and thus are different; they are created to complement and complete one another. Maston feels that perhaps some of the problems that have arisen in contemporary homes and in society stem from the fact that men and women have become too competitive with one another. In his words:

> God does not judge as people judge. . . . It may be that from God's viewpoint, the role of wife and mother is superior to any other role for a woman and may be more important than the typical role of the man and husband.
> . . . Let us repeat, however, that differential in roles does not mean primary and secondary or superior and inferior roles.[30]

Maston deals effectively with the controversial subject of "equality and submission" in marriage.[31] First he discusses the concept of freedom in Christ, but he explains then that in all human relations "the fullest freedom comes through mutual submission and unselfish devotion and service to and for one another."[32] This may mean that we will need to limit our own freedom for the sake of others' welfare.

Maston includes a rather extensive discussion of the vitally important passage on marriage found in Ephesians 5:21-33. I believe that the primary topic dealt with here is mutual responsibility. In the past, perhaps to at least partly accommodate to cultural practices and customs, this passage was con-

---

[28]Paul K. Jewett, *Man and Male and Female: A Study in Sexual Relationships from a Theological Point of View* (Grand Rapids: Eerdmans, 1975) 14, cited by Maston and Tillman, 164-65.

[29]Maston and Tillman, *The Bible and Family,* 165.

[30]Ibid., 168.

[31]Ibid., 168-76.

[32]Ibid., 171-72.

sidered by most interpreters to begin with verse 22, which reads: "Wives, submit yourselves unto your own husbands, as unto the Lord." Probably one key reason for beginning the passage with verse 22 is that many editions of the King James Version of the Bible placed a paragraph symbol immediately in front of the verse. Thus, many readers and no few interpreters grouped verse 21, which reads, "Submitting yourselves to one *another* in the fear of God," (author's italics) with the preceding passage that discusses practices of worship.

Verse 21 more logically belongs, however, with the passage on marriage that follows for two principal reasons: (1) verse 22 does not actually contain a verb in a number of the best Greek manuscripts; thus, translators take the verb "submit" in verse 22, from the participle "submitting" in verse 21; and (2) verse 21 is a general principle that Paul uses to apply to three types of human relations that follow immediately: husbands and wives (5:22-31), parents and children (6:1-4), and employers and employees (6:5-9).

Thus, Paul begins his counsel by stating that in marriage, as well as in other types of human relationships, the *principle of mutual submission* should prevail. Surely this principle, as applied to marriage, should not be surprising to Christians. The apostle states it in other passages: "Let nothing be done through strife or vainglory; but in lowliness of mind let each esteem other better than themselves" (Phil. 2:3); and "Be kindly affectioned one to another with brotherly love; in honor preferring one another" (Rom. 12:10). He uses the Savior himself as the example when he states that believers should have the spirit of Christ who "made himself of no reputation and took upon him the form of a servant" (Phil. 2:7). Jesus also reminded his followers that they, like he, were "not to be ministered unto but to minister" (Matt. 20:28). Do these principles of servanthood and submission not apply in the home as well as outside it?

In what way today might a husband find the need for submitting to his wife? Perhaps, particularly if she works outside the home or has small children, by helping to perform some of those tasks carried out in the kitchen or the nursery. And how might a wife be called on to submit to her husband? Perhaps, particularly if her husband is the chief wage earner in the family, by being willing to move away from her parents and relatives, if his job calls for it. Certainly to listen patiently and with understanding to each other is a type of submission on the part of spouses, especially at the end of a busy, tiring day. Yet, it is so important and necessary.

There is, however, a second principle in this passage—the *principle of essential authority*. Mutual submission is not meant to supplant essential authority. Without clear lines of ultimate authority, confusion or even chaos can result, whether it be in society or in a home. Just as there are employers and employees, governors and the governed, so there must be heads of households as well as those who comprise them. Paul suggests that the person who should accept this responsibility is the husband.

Being the head of a home is no easy task. It requires continual decision making. The wise manager soon learns that he needs to consult often with those who are also affected by his decisions. He may not always follow the advice of his wife, and perhaps the children if they are older, but more co-operation is usually obtained if he has at least consulted them. Leslie and Korman report that most American marriages are of this type today.[33] In some areas, the husband may need to delegate authority (in say, cooking or even handling the checkbook) to take advantage of the best skills and abilities of each spouse. If, for some reason, the husband does not accept his responsi-bility (for example, in religious matters or helping to discipline the children), then the wife will obviously have to assume it. In cases of differences of opin-ion, someone needs to accept the responsibility for the final choice, someone needs to be the tie-breaker; and Paul suggests that this should be the husband.

In verses 22-24 the apostle advises and appeals to wives to submit, sub-ject, or adapt themselves voluntarily to their husbands, just as they do when they choose to serve the Lord. Nothing servile, slavish, or menial is implied here; rather, a willing cooperation and yielding is given in the same way that the body of Christ, his Church, follows his leadership. Maston adds his clar-ification to the meaning of this requested submission:

> There are at least two *kinds of subjection:* as inferior to a superior or an equal to an equal. It is clear from the biblical teachings in general that the subjection spoken of by Paul and Peter [1 Peter 2:13] was an equal to an equal.
>
> Also, the submission of one person to another could be involuntary or voluntary. It is clear in the passage in Ephesians 5 that whatever submission was enjoined on wives was voluntary. Paul did not say, "Husbands see that your wives are submissive," but rather, "Wives, be subject to your hus-bands" (v. 22) and "as to the Lord."[34]

In the remaining verses of chapter 5, Paul advises the husband of his re-sponsibility to his wife. He is to love her in at least two very special ways: (1) "as Christ loved the Church," that is, sacrificially and unselfishly; and (2) as the husband loves himself. Maston reminds us that the word used here for love is the "distinctly New Testament term *agape,* the highest form of love. It is the type of love that God has for us, self-giving, self-sacrificial love that reaches out to another even when there is no reciprocation. What wife would have a problem subordinating herself to a husband who practices this

---

[33]Leslie and Korman, *The Family,* 501.

[34]Maston and Tillman, *The Bible and Family,* 171-72.

type of love toward her? Maston says, " 'As Christ loved' should be the standard for every Christian husband in every relation with his wife . . . this whole concept will necessitate a self-control or denial of self that at least would approximate submission or subordination."[35]

Thus, there is to be a mutual submission in marriage; the wife is to submit her will by respecting the final decisions of her husband, and he is to submit his own will to doing what is best for his wife, because he loves her as Christ loves (v. 33). A successful marriage requires mutual respect and appreciation. As Maston has often said to his students, "It is like the violin and the bow;" neither is complete without the other; however, cooperating together, ecstasy can be the outcome.

Actually, the biblical goal for marriage is not happiness; it is oneness or unity, the concept of "one flesh," or a blending of two personalities into one. This oneness is never sameness, for there is always a potential for greater richness with diversity. Happiness results as a byproduct of unity in marriage and is made possible as each partner submits to the will of him who brought them into being. Finally, it is interesting to note here what Leslie and Korman state as a summary of research on the topic of "marital power" in modern American marriages:

> Recent studies show most marriages to have a fairly equal distribution of power, with some couples emphasizing autonomous decision making and others emphasizing joint decision making. Surprisingly, husband-dominated marriages have about as many high-happiness ratings as do egalitarian ones. Wife-dominated marriages have a much smaller percentage of very satisfactory relationships. Marriages in which one partner dominates the other are few in number however.[36]

PARENTS AND CHILDREN

Maston deals with parents and children as a relationship that is always reciprocal. For convenience, however, he first discusses parents' responsibilities to children and then the converse.

Maston says the Bible assumes that parents will have children, if they are physically able. He agrees that ordinarily couples should have children, and will deny themselves part of God's intention for them if they do not. However, he does state that "there may be some who should not have children."[37]

---

[35]Ibid., 172.

[36]Leslie and Korman, *The Family,* 501.

[37]Maston and Tillman, *The Bible and Family,* 225.

He also states that every child has the inherent right to be wanted and planned for.

Parents are responsible to God for every child. The child should be given back to God for him to use as he wills. The Bible teaches that parents are to love, discipline, teach or train, and dedicate their children. Maston says that there is "no necessary conflict" between love and discipline. "When discipline is properly administered it can and will be an expression of love."[38] A few other choice comments of Maston on this topic follow:

> The purpose of discipline is that he may mature into a person who can discipline himself. In order for this to be accomplished, the child must understand the purpose of the discipline and believe in its fairness.
>
> Also, children cannot mature into well-disciplined persons unless they are led increasingly to make their own decisions.
>
> The effectiveness of punishment depends more on its consistency and the child's understanding the reason for the punishment than on its severity.
>
> [Parents] cannot expect to have well-disciplined children unless they themselves are well-disciplined.
>
> The best discipline is largely unconscious, primarily caught rather than taught.
>
> Be positive more than negative in approach to and interpretation of the Christian life . . . the chief test of the Christian is positive: how much he exemplifies in his life the teachings and spirit of Christ.[39]

Maston also reminds us that not to discipline is not to love. God certainly disciplines his children. However, only discipline that is motivated by love will be highly effective (Prov. 3:11-12). The fruit of discipline is whether the child has learned from it, but Maston makes the point that parents as well as children can learn from necessary discipline.[40]

The chief responsibilities of children to parents is to honor (reverence or respect) them, obey them, and provide for them. Even if parents are not always worthy of honor, children should respect parenthood itself enough not to be severely critical of their parents.

Obedience to parents is not to come before obedience to God, but it is to take a high priority in one's life, especially while one still lives at home. Providing for one's parents, particularly in their older years is a clear responsibility. Maston has an extensive discussion of the passage where the Pharisees were failing to fulfill their responsibilities to their parents in a financial sense (Matt. 15:1-9).[41]

---

[38]T. B. Maston, *The Conscience of a Christian* (Waco TX: Word Books, 1971) 81.

[39]Ibid., 81-84.

[40]Maston and Tillman, *The Bible and Family,* 228.

[41]Ibid., 245.

Maston, in his major book on the family, devotes an entire chapter to older adults. In it he deals with topics such as "Age and Aging," "Elders," the qualities of the aging, and the attitudes the Bible exhorts us to have toward senior adults. He concludes the chapter with an extremely practical discussion of "Their Crises." In his brief discussion on death, one of the best I have discovered to date, he exhibits his faith:

> It may be wise for all of us to remember that death is like a swinging door. Such a door provides a way in, as well as a way out. We may not know much about what awaits us on the other side, but we do know Who waits for us. He will be there and if he is there, that will be enough. We can rest in and on that assurance.[42]

SINGLE ADULTS

T. B. Maston has spent much of his life working with and relating to single adults. He taught for over forty years at Southwestern Baptist Theological Seminary and chose to spend time counseling and relating closely to students. He continues to follow the lives of many of his students, particularly those who majored in Christian ethics under him. He and his wife invited students into their home often. The first book he wrote, to my knowledge, was a book on recreation in the church and it was widely used by young people. One of Maston's most consistent activities during retirement has been that of speaking to the orientation for Southern Baptist journeymen, a group of largely single adults. Maston, through the years, has been a frequent speaker on college campuses, and even as a very "mature" adult (one of his expressions while speaking to such groups), he holds the attention of his youthful audiences.

Maston's treatment of the topic "Single Adults" in his book on the family encompasses the Bible's discussion of the widowed, the divorced (although an entire chapter is devoted to them elsewhere), and the never married. It is worth noting at this point that these three groups in American society now constitute forty percent of all persons aged fifteen and older.[43] The percentage could go higher if present trends of increasing longevity, postponing the age for marriage, and the demand for increasing education on the part of females continue in the United States.

The best way to summarize Maston's views on single adulthood would be to quote several of his conclusions at the end of his chapter:

---

[42]Ibid., 153.

[43]Edward L. Kain, "Surprising Singles," *American Demographics* (August 1984) 16.

Neither marriage nor singleness is a superior state. . . . Both are treated
with honor when perceived as a part of one's calling by and relationship to
God.

The church can aid [the divorced and widowed] in dealing with the en-
suing grief process which follows the break in a relationship.

Research shows that the drive for sexual relations, unlike that for food,
can be sublimated.

The establishment of a pattern of discovering fellowship with God . . .
can be a great source of strength in times of temptations and pressures.

More attention needs to be given to how single adults . . . can be ministered to and in turn can minister in and through the church to others in
need.[44]

SEX AND SEXUAL RELATIONS

Space will not permit an extensive treatment even of Maston's discussion
of the topic of sex in his major work on the family. Only a few of the principal
emphases will be included.

Maston stresses that the Bible teaches that sex is inherently good and is
God-given. The idea that sex is evil entered Christian theology not from Jew-
ish thought or biblical teaching but through some of the forms of Greek philosophy. The Jews had a wholistic view of humanity, and the concept of
"flesh" included the entire personality. Sexual union then is not meant to be
exclusively physical; rather it is intended to involve and symbolize the union
of two persons. The biblical concept of "knowing" the other person in the
sense of intercourse correctly communicates God's intention that intercourse
bring about a deeper and fuller level of understanding and affection for married partners.

Maston has a rather extended discussion of the biblical teaching concerning homosexuality. He first clarifies that the Bible deals with overt homosexual behavior, not as a mere state of mind or homosexual "orientation."
Sexual intercourse is intended only for a monogamous heterosexual union of
husband and wife. This means that the practice of homosexuality is sin.
Nevertheless, there is always hope for salvation and a change of practice. Also,
if one simply has a homosexual orientation, he or she may refrain from actual
practice just as the heterosexual is expected to refrain from fornication or
adultery. To fail to do so is also to sin, and one is not condemned any greater
than the other. Both were equally punished by death in the Old Testament.

Maston also has some direct words of caution to Christians concerning
the tendency to judge homosexuals harshly:

---

[44]Maston and Tillman, *The Bible and Family,* 129.

Church members should beware of developing self-righteous, pharisaical attitudes toward the homosexual or any other particular type of sinner. After all, the most scathing denunciations by Jesus were reserved for self-righteous sinners.[45]

He concludes the chapter by emphasizing again that Jesus made sin primarily inner. The unsaved are not the only sinners; the children of God are still in that category also.

DIVORCE AND REMARRIAGE

Maston, as always, takes a nonjudgmental, compassionate but straightforward approach to the delicate and difficult topic of divorce. After clarifying that the Bible does not have a systematic manner in which it discusses divorce and contains more information in passages that simply offer answers to questions that were posed, Maston makes some important initial statements that set the stage for his treatment of the topic. He declares that since divorce falls short of God's purpose for marriage, it involves sin. However, one should not be dogmatic "about what Jesus and/or Paul would say concerning complex situations faced by some husbands and wives in the contemporary world."[46]

Maston doubts that Jesus was legislating when he uttered the statements concerning the questions asked him on divorce. Divorce is sin, but forgiveness is certainly available. Both parties should seek forgiveness and grant it also. Remarriage should not be considered until there is genuine repentance and a willingness to forgive as well.

Maston underscores again the importance of forgiveness on the part of church members toward those who are divorcees. There should be a desire to be helpful to them, as divorce usually involves a grieving process similar to when a loved one is lost in death. On the other hand, the church should guard against accommodating itself too much to its culture and the contemporary situation of this day. With respect to remarriage, this—as with all decisions of importance—should be submitted to the will of God and entered into only after much prayerful consideration.

---

[45]Ibid., 195.

[46]Ibid., 204.

CONCLUSION

T. B. Maston's treatment of family life has been expansive. As with other areas of ethics, Maston has provided foundational ideas. In addition, he has pointed toward horizons that must yet be explored.

BLACK AMERICA: FROM BAD NEWS TO GOOD NEWS/BAD NEWS

JOHN A. WOOD
BAYLOR UNIVERSITY
WACO TEXAS

INTRODUCTION

When T. B. Maston began to make his prophetic statements on race in the 1940s and 1950s,[1] blacks in America were denied basic civil and human rights. Although no longer slaves, in a real sense conditions for many were little better than those during slavery. A black writer states it in stronger terms: "For all black people some of the time, and for most southern blacks all the time, it was worse than anarchy. It was war."[2] Blacks were reduced to a "status of slavery without chains."[3] To be sure, some blacks had attained a

---

[1]See especially *The Christian in the Modern World* (Nashville: Broadman, 1952) ch. 4, and *Christianity and World Issues* (New York: Macmillan, 1957) ch. 4. Dr. Maston's large treatments on race are found in *Segregation and Desegregation: A Christian Approach* (New York: Macmillan, 1959) and *The Bible and Race* (Nashville: Broadman, 1959). His earliest book on the subject was a brief treatment entitled *Of One: A Study of Christian Principles and Race Relations* (Atlanta: Home Mission Board, 1946). To put it mildly, Dr. Maston's views were not acceptable to many Southern Baptists, but his strong biblical basis silenced his critics.

[2]Derrick A. Bell, Jr., "The Racial Imperative in American Law," *The Age of Segregation: Race Relations in the South, 1890-1945* (Jackson MS: University of Mississippi, 1978) 3.

[3]Ibid., 17.

measure of financial security and status in the community, primarily ministers, funeral home directors, medical personnel, and owners of small busi-
nesses. But for the great majority intimidation and degradation were the order
of the day. Separate accommodations were a constant source of humiliation
and inconvenience. ''For Whites Only'' signs were insidious reminders that
blacks were second-class citizens. Whites may have divided blacks into
''coloreds'' (good Negroes) and ''niggers'' (bad Negroes), but treatment was
essentially the same.

Political disenfranciement meant that blacks had no power to redress
wrongs. Although legally able to vote, most feared retaliation if they did vote,
except for those who had been bought off or forced to vote for a particular
candidate.

Educational opportunities were inferior at all levels. Consistently, segregation meant that the lions share of limited public funds for education went
to white schools.

To a high school student today, all this sounds like ancient history. Why?
Because the Civil Rights Movement brought about rapid social change in many
areas. The situation in the mid-1980s is substantially different from the 1940s
and 1950s. Many of the issues addressed by Dr. Maston have been resolved,
at least to some extent. The issues today, however, are more blurred and
complex, containing a mixture of racial and nonracial dimensions. There is
both good news and bad news.

GOOD NEWS

Since Dr. Maston's efforts to educate Southern Baptists on racial issues,
there have been some clear gains for black Americans.[4]

---

[4]Racial issues are changing dramatically in the United States, particularly due to the rapid
increase in the Hispanic population. This paper will attempt, however, to focus primarily on
black America. The terms ''race relations'' and ''racial justice'' will be used interchangeably.
Gayraud Wilmore has made an interesting observation regarding the different races in ''The
Path Toward Racial Justice,'' *Journal of Presbyterian History* (Spring 1983): 112.

It is doubtless a caricature of the real situation, but it may be near the truth that
what the Native Americans want are their treaty rights and to be simply left alone;
what the Asian Americans want is a new opportunity to benefit from American capitalism while holding on to their traditional family system; what the Hispanics want
is unity among bitterly contesting national groupings and recognition of their common language and culture; what the blacks want is power; and what the whites want
is to hold on to it for as long as possible. It is clear that no one solution will serve
the interest of all groups and in many instances the non-white groups stand in each
other's ways vis-a-vis the white males, who continue to control the polity and the
dominant institutions of the society.

1. The Jim Crow laws, which were so humiliating to blacks, have been nullified. The psychological benefits of this change were enormous. It enabled blacks to experience a sense of pride and dignity. They could move about in society freely and without embarrassment. The more overt forms of racism were removed rather rapidly.

2. There have been notable gains in the securing of political power. Most noteworthy has been the election of black mayors in such cities as Atlanta, Birmingham, Chicago, Detroit, Los Angeles, and Philadelphia.[5] Virtually no progress has been made in the U.S. Senate, but the House has seen several blacks rise to prominence. When William Gray was elected chairman of the House Appropriations Committee in 1984, it was said that he thereby became the most powerful politician in black history. Although blacks remain statistically underrepresented in the total elective offices,[6] a mere two decades ago only a few visionary blacks could have dreamed that blacks would have come this far.

3. A black middle class has emerged. Blacks are seen in places where they were not found a few decades ago. Some are even found in the so-called Yuppie (young urban professionals) movement. These blacks project a totally different image than did their predecessors. Today there are different role models for young blacks to emulate.

4. In education the gains are more ambiguous but nonetheless real. The results of the desegregation of public schools are fiercely debated, but few deny that it has resulted in better educational opportunities for many blacks. More blacks are graduating from high school and going on to college. Several black colleges and universities flourish and previously all-white public and private institutions have substantial numbers of blacks attending.

5. Possibly the area of progress most readily recognized is in athletics. Blacks dominate many sports today. The inroads made into prizefighting in the days of Jack Johnson and Joe Louis have expanded into football, baseball, and basketball. Many predominately white colleges, for example, field a near totally black basketball team. Professional sports have become an avenue for several blacks to make small fortunes.

---

[5]Note the observation of William J. Wilson, *The Declining Significance of Race* (Chicago: University Press, 1978) 139: "The dilemma to urban blacks is that they are gaining political influence in large urban areas . . . at the very time when the political power and influence of the cities are on the wane."

[6]In 1970 there were 1,469 black elected officials (BEO); in 1980 there were 4,912 BEOs—according to Milton Morris, *Black Electorial Participation and the Distribution of Public Benefits* (Washington DC: Brookings Institute, 1982) 177.

BAD NEWS

Generally social change affecting minorities comes about slowly and in increments, unless there is a violent overthrow of the system. Violence, planned and spontaneous, and the threat of violence, played a role in the Civil Rights Movement. But the major advances came through nonviolence. Progress on many fronts has been substantial. But, as we reach the mid-1980s there are still many unresolved issues. There are some serious, some would say frightening, signs on the horizon.

1. Possibly the most serious crisis facing black Americans is the disintegration of the family unit. The systematic destruction of the black family in the slavery era has borne bitter fruit. In short, the black family has not recovered from the unprecedented attack on the family that was unabated for three hundred years. Furthermore, the enormous pressure on the modern nuclear family has severely strained families of all races. Just when blacks were entering into an opportunity to start with new building blocks in society, they were hampered by the breakup of the family. There is an alarming increase in unwed black mothers. Nearly one-half of all black families are headed by females.[7] Many single mothers perform admirably under these stressful conditions, but it nonetheless is hard to over-emphasize the damage done to the coming generation. The presence of extended family members has cushioned the blow for some, but an extremely serious problem exists. Working mothers, themselves poor and uneducated, are handicapped when it comes to motivating and disciplining children. Many school teachers complain that they can count on little cooperation from many black homes in the education of their children.

2. To focus more specifically on education, we note that white flight to suburbs continues in many places so that in some major cities blacks and other minorities comprise the majority of students. A shrinking tax base means less money for education. In addition, segregation occurs within some schools. That is, in an effort to stem the flight of whites from the public schools, many districts have initiated ''gifted and talented'' programs, which are overwhelmingly white. Many dedicated teachers, both black and white, are frustrated in their attempts to educate a new generation of blacks. To be sure, there are oases in the desert. Many are, and will be, better educated than their parents, but for many the outlook is bleak. Social promotions and dropouts continue and this will have a deleterious effect on future black America.

---

[7]Female-headed households jumped from 28 percent in 1970 to 41 percent in 1982, *American Black Population 1970-1982: A Statistical View* (Washington DC: US Department of Commerce Bureau of the Census, 1982) 16f.

The emotional issue of busing has subsided somewhat as the focus is more on what happens to the children once they arrive at school. Some whites feel threatened by low-income blacks, some of whom have been raised in an atmosphere of violence.

3. Related to the issue of education is the earlier mentioned emphasis on athletics. Athletics appear to be an avenue for some to make money without reliance upon an education. While it is true that several blacks have become rich due to their athletic abilities, it has a negative side. Jesse Jackson and other black leaders decry this emphasis on sports, pointing out that the percentage of those who "make it big" is small indeed. Though the overwhelming majority of black athletes do not achieve professional status, these few serve as major role models for countless youth who dream of stardom and wealth. The result is a building of unrealistic expectations and a neglect of "mental athletics," which alone holds the key to emancipation from poverty and mediocrity.

4. Crime continues to plague many black communities. Several years ago *Ebony* magazine devoted an entire issue to this matter.[8] *Ebony* caused a stir with its candid statements. The sad truth, the periodical noted, is that black on black crime is alarmingly high.[9] Drug abuse is related to this problem. Drugs were a serious problem in black communities long before they found their way into white communities. In earlier days, drugs proved a temporary relief for blacks who saw no way out of the ghetto. This is still true for many. In addition, the drug pusher has provided a role model, however sinister and misguided, to young blacks who see drug dealing as a way to escape poverty.

5. In the economic area it has already been noted that a new middle class has emerged. Civil Rights legislation and Affirmative Action programs enabled prepared blacks to enter into the economic mainstream. But, as Wilmore has noted, "Incremental gains by the black middle class during the past ten years tend to distort a true picture of the situation. We have today a permanent and growing black underclass, more wretched and neglected, more alienated than at any previous time in our history."[10]

Unemployment rates among blacks, particularly young blacks, is substantially higher than among their white counterparts. To add to the problem, Bayard Rustin considers "the plight of black Americans today is more and more the consequences of important nonracist, structural features of our

---

[8]*Ebony* (August 1979).

[9]Ibid., 36, 42, 44.

[10]Wilmore, "The Path," 112f. But note the growth of nonwhites in selected jobs from 1972-1982 in The *New York Times,* 10 March 1985, E8.

economy.''[11] Rustin, no doubt, is thinking of the major shifts in our economy noted in John Naisbitt's bestselling *Megatrends,* for example, the elimination of many jobs in the steel and automotive industries, the decline in labor-intensive industries due to automation, the decline in the size of public sector employment, and so forth.[12] These changes have caught large numbers of blacks unprepared. Many jobs occupied by blacks have, and will, become obsolete. There is fear that some will not obtain the skills to compete in the new economic ball game.

6. Prejudice, or attitudinal racism, appears to be on the upswing. Jesse Jackson noted in 1980 that ''Racism has become fashionable again and feelings of guilt toward blacks have turned to feelings of hostility. This country has taken a definite swing toward fascism.''[13] Many who were committed to social justice in the 1960s and 1970s have noted a reversal in racial attitudes among their children.

These activists, who experienced a generation gap with their parents, now experience it with their children. Those who supported Civil Rights now see their children developing racist attitudes as a result of their experiences with blacks. What used to be common fistfights in junior high and high school now often have racial overtones. Some middle class white teens have their first close contact with poor blacks who have lived in a violent subculture. Without a proper understanding of the history and causes of this problem, racial attitudes inevitably become negative.

Racist attitudes in their most distressing form are seen in the persistence, in some quarters, of a fairly vigorous Ku Klux Klan. Observers have noted that the Klan movement tends to follow a pattern of depressed numbers and then resurgence.[14] But the persistent presence of the Klan and of the various factions of the Neo-Nazi movement indicate a substratum of racism in America that will not go away.

Although these groups remain on the fringes of society, they are capable of producing a climate of fear and intimidation in some communities. It is a part of what George Kelsey noted in his classic work *Racism and the Christian Understanding of Man:* ''Man tends to glorify and exalt himself on the

---

[11]Bayard Rustin, ''Civil Rights: Twenty Years Later,'' *Newsweek* (August 29, 1983): 11.

[12]John Naisbitt, *Megatrends* (New York: Warner Books, 1982) esp. Ch. 1.

[13]Cited in Wilmore, ''The Path,'' 114.

[14]Janet Eyler and Ronald E. Galbraith, *How Is It Possible: An Examination of the KKK* (Nashville: The Nashville Panel, 1980). They note a twenty-year cycle pattern, p. 7. See also the entire issue of *Engage/Social Action* (September 1981): 10-56.

strength of his exclusive associations and connections—the nation, the race, the party, the profession."[15]

Beyond the Klan's approach, Alan Davies has noted the emergence of a new and subtle mode of race-thinking:

> Who are the new race-thinkers? They are found among politicians, political philosophers, and possibly even scientists in both Europe and North America, especially the defenders of hereditarian doctrines of human difference. They are the heirs of Herbert Spencer, Sir Francis Galton, and the Social Darwinists, which, in spite of the Nazi epoch, still continue to mold part of the contemporary scientific mind. They tend to believe that innate intelligence and other personal attributes are closely related to the socioeconomic status of the various segments of society as determining factors, and hint that the way things are is also the way things should be.[16]

Most of Davies's research centers on the French neo-Gallist movement, but he cites authors whose works are influential in America, including Arthur Jensen, Konrad Lorenz, Robert Ardrey, and Desmond Morris. These authors provide some pseudointellectual racists a basis upon which to mold a respectable racism. This will chip away at some of the gains in the area of attitudinal racism.[17]

The influx of other minorities in some parts of the country appears to have exacerbated racist attitudes. Some whites seem to have developed a siege mentality. Trying to understand and deal with blacks was difficult enough for these folks, but now other ethnic groups, whose cultures are even more difficult to understand, are making their presence known. It is commonly accepted that Hispanics will become the largest minority in the U.S. in the next few decades and, if our history is any indiction, this will lead to further conflicts within communities.[18]

---

[15]George Kelsey, *Racism and the Christian Understanding of Man* (New York: Charles Scribner's Sons, 1965) 78.

[16]Alan Davies, "The Politics of the Living: A Case Study in Scientific Neo-racism," *Journal of Religious Thought* (Fall-Winter 1982-1983): 26. See also Gaspar B. Largella, "The Politics of Genetic Inequality: Public Policy Considerations for the Pastor," *Church and Society* (September/October 1982): 79-89.

[17]"Freedom is celebrated as the distinguishing mark of humanity and it has genetic and biological roots. Racial mixture is bad because it interferes with homogeneous culture and the cohesion it should have." In a speech by Alan Davies at the annual meeting of the Society of Christian Ethics, Atlanta, Georgia, 19 January 1985.

[18]James Hargett in *The Bulletin of the Martin Luther King Fellows, Inc.* (Spring 1980) 1-4, 7, comments:

> The Asians . . . seem to arrive here with the entrepreneurial skills to get ahead regardless of political power or land ownership . . . Korean and Mexican gas stations

Evidence of resistance to newcomers to communities, even when they are white, is seen in several put-down bumper stickers such as "We're glad you visited Texas—now go home!" or "We don't care how you did it up North!" If these regional animosities resurface regularly, what can be expected when unfamiliar minorities gain in population? Furthermore, there is some evidence that racial jokes are once again becoming more socially acceptable, following a decline during and immediately after the height of the Civil Rights Movement.

The persistence and depth of this racism may point beyond mere sociological analysis. It may confirm Joseph Washington's belief that there exists in this country a deep-seated "demonic affliction" that he calls a "religion of antiblackness."[19]

> Antiblackness (unlike prejudice, slavery, discrimination, segregation) continues nearly unabated from generation to generation. Antiblackness has not suffered defeat although it has encountered setbacks. When checked in one human area or another, it finds refuge and unmatched growth in another dark region of our social milieu . . . In our lifetime, nowhere has this devil spirit demonstrated its extra human power more extensively and ruthlessly than in bringing the Civil Rights Movement to an abrupt impasse.[20]

The work of Lawrence Kohlberg of Harvard may provide some insights into attitudinal racism and the prospects for change. Kohlberg has postulated six stages of moral development."[21] Each person goes through the same stages in the same order, although some may get "stuck" at one stage and never progress to the next.

---

and groceries in Los Angeles are already showing this strong tendency, to say nothing of the Cuban dominance of retail outlets in Miami. Even the underworld in the ghetto has been taken over, and the dope traffic brought under the control of non-white, non-black operators in black communities in Chicago, New York, and Los Angeles. With this acceptance of Third World overlords, black confidence in blacks will take a turn for the worse, unless something significant is done to reverse the trend.

Interestingly enough, however, the number of mixed marriages rose from 310,000 in 1970 to 613,000 in 1980. "Children of the Rainbow," *Newsweek* (19 November 1984): 120. For an insightful study on the problems faced by Mexican-Americans see Samuel J. Surace, "Achievement, Discrimination, and Mexican-Americans," *Comparative Study of Society and History* (April 1982): 315-39.

[19]Joseph R. Washington, Jr., "The Religion of Antiblackness," *Theology Today* (July 1981): 146.

[20]Ibid., 147.

[21]Lawrence Kohlberg, *The Philosophy of Moral Development* (New York: Harper & Row, 1981) 23.

Stage one may be called the ''obedience and punishment'' stage. The primary motivation for doing what is right is to avoid punishment. According to Kohlberg, everyone begins at this stage.

Stage two may be referred to as the ''individualism and reciprocity'' stage. Here the criterion of what is right is that of the greatest good for the individual making the decision. In order to achieve this good a person often must enter into agreements with others, but self-interest is still the motive for entering into these ''deals.''

Stage three is called by Kohlberg the ''interpersonal conformity'' stage. What is right will be determined by what is expected of one by people close to him or by people generally. The individual wants to be a good member of the team and will act accordingly.

Stage four is the ''social system'' of ''law and order'' stage. Morality is comprised of doing one's duty or obeying the rules. *Kolberg's view is that most American adults are fixated at this stage.* A major motive for persons at this stage is to keep society going.

Stage five is the ''social contract'' stage. This stage presupposes some kind of independent reflection on morality. A person at this stage recognizes that there are moral values that are independent from the accepted values of society. Here a person asks ''What is best for everyone on the whole?'' or ''What could all of us in principle agree to?''

Stage six is the highest stage and is called the stage of ''universal ethical principles.'' The few persons who reach this stage hold to such principles as equality, human rights, and respect for the intrinsic dignity of all human beings. Gandhi and Dr. Martin Luther King, Jr. reached this stage.[22]

For our purposes we must examine the outlook for race relations and racial justice if Kohlberg is correct that most Americans are fixated at stage four. It is easy to see how Southern whites once defended a segregation that represented the proper social system and had the backing of the law. Dr. King, operating out of stage six, did not bring society out of lower stages merely because the legal basis for segregation was destroyed. If most people remain in stage four, they have yet to engage in serious reflection on morality in race relations, which would occur in stage five or six. Racist attitudes are compatible with the moral reasoning of stages one through four. Leaders, operating out of stage five or six, may bring about structural changes in society through the force of their personalities or through political power. But if these changes antagonize the many who remain in lower stages, serious difficulties arise. This seems to illustrate what happened following the substantial changes

---

[22]Parts of the foregoing discussion on Kohlberg are following closely an unpublished manuscript on *Business Values* by Warren French and John Granrose.

brought about by Civil Rights legislation. It appears certain that issues of racial justice will not be on the agenda for those operating in stages one through four. Only those in stages five and six and willing to bring to bear universal moral principles on the complex problems of racial justice will consider such problems.

Therefore, if Kohlberg is correct, the moral reasoning level of the general American public ensures that the road to racial justice will be long and enormously difficult. Indeed, one may go so far as to insist that racial justice is *impossible* in a nation stuck in conventional levels of moral development.[23]

OTHER CONTRIBUTING FACTORS

There are several current sociocultural phenomena that have an impact on racial issues.

1. There is a withdrawing into privatized religion. Many feel the need for a religious experience but are not guided into the moral and social implications of their religious beliefs. Part of this may be attributed to a reaction to what was perceived as undue religious involvement in racial and peace issues in the 1960s and 1970s. Many of a conservative religious persuasion did not appreciate the "liberals" who promoted busing, affirmative action, and disarmament, but their voices were muted because of the mood of the times. As this mood changed, these people were able to hold on to their religious belief and denounce many of the goals and programs designed to promote racial justice.[24]

2. This tendency toward privatized religion dovetails with the worldwide resurgence of conservatism that has had a great impact on the drive for racial justice. There is a longing to go back to the good old days of the Eisenhower era when the United States ruled the world and minorities were in their proper places. It is supposed that the family was strong, that religious beliefs dominated the institutions of society, and that everyone was happy with the way things were.

---

[23]This reminds one of the statement by the German professor Theodor Adorno: "Of the world as it exists, one cannot be enough afraid," cited in Jonathon Green, *International Dictionary of Contemporary Quotations* (New York: Morrow, 1982) 1.

[24]This is closely allied with the over-emphasis in some circles on the Second Coming of Christ. One pastor said that all this Armageddon talk is "almost a prayer for escape, asking for a self-fulfilling of prophecy." A New Testament scholar said such talk is "the urge to solve one's own personal or communal problems by imagining or planning the destruction of the world," cited in Martin Marty's *Context* (15 December 1984): 5.

Although this picture greatly oversimplifies that period of time, there is some truth to it. Mind-altering drugs were not a serious problem among youth. The sexual revolution had not taken place. Sex and violence were not the standard fare for television and movies. All of these changes began to occur as the racial revolution was unfolding and many seemed to identify these changes with the Civil Rights Movement. Thus, the Civil Rights Movement was blamed for many of these changes that threatened whites. This "scapegoat" tendency is in addition to the familiar "white backlash" that followed closely on the heels of the Civil Rights Movement.

Furthermore, conservatives who did not withdraw from the public arena, set out a new moral agenda that decidedly did not include racial justice. Abortion, long a central concern of Roman Catholics, became the prime moral concern for many conservatives. Prayer in the public schools, part of the effort to turn back the clock to an earlier era, gained wide attention. Some feel that there are racist overtones to this new moral agenda. The concern over violence and disrespect in the public schools paralleled the entry of minorities into desegregated schools. Therefore, the reason for the problems in public education is minority participation. Therefore, to "conserve" the values of former days, segregation academies blossomed and continue to multiply.

An intriguing aspect of this move toward conservatism is the support given to it by a new breed of black intellectuals. In spite of the substantial differences in their views, such scholars as William J. Wilson, Thomas Sowell, Walter Williams, and Derrick Bell, Jr., avoid generalized indictments of American society and dispute purely racial explanations of the plight of poor blacks.[25]

Wilson believes that "even if all racial discrimination in labor-market practices were eliminated tomorrow, economic conditions would not significantly improve because of structural barriers to decent jobs."[26] Wilson is encouraged concerning college-educated blacks who receive roughly the same salaries as their white counterparts, but notes that the plight of young, poor blacks is worsening. But he sees this more of a class problem than a race problem.[27]

Williams appears to support the Reagan administration's policies by insisting that the problem of poor blacks has resulted from government interference and from organized labor. He supports the repeal of the minimum wage

---

[25]Murray Friedman, "The New Black Intellectuals," *Commentary* (June 1980): 47.

[26]Wilson, *The Declining Significance of Race,* 21-23.

[27]Friedman, "The New Black Intellectuals," 48.

law which, he maintains, mitigates against black youth.[28] He also argues strongly for a free market.[29]

Bell has attacked the view that school integration is the cure-all for black advancement. While not opposed to integration as such, he argues that the focus should be on providing high-quality education in predominately black schools.[30]

Sowell, possibly the best known of these scholars, is opposed to white liberals and black extremists who, he feels, have made things worse for blacks. In the conclusion of his excellent book on *Race and Economics,* he states:

> Perhaps the greatest dilemma in attempts to raise ethnic minority income is that those methods which have historically proved successful—self-reliance, work skills, education, business experience—are all slow developing, while those methods which are direct and immediate—job quotas, charity, subsidies, preferential treatment—tend to undermine self-reliance and pride of achievement in the long run.[31]

These writers have sparked a lively and oftentimes heated debate. They often find themselves in near total disagreement with those who have exercised leadership among blacks for decades. Although this is a needed debate, because it raises important issues, it has enabled some whites to engage in a "divide and conquer" technique, which, for all intents and purposes, mutes voices for change and leads to a laissez-faire attitude on matters of racial justice.

3. Although the impact on racial concerns is hard to measure, there seems to be a new wave of hedonism and selfishness in the country.[32] Abigail

---

[28]Walter Williams, "Government Sanctioned Restraints on Minorities," *Policy Review* (Fall 1977): 15.

[29]Ibid., 28-30. But Williams recently spoke in favor of Affirmative Action: "Civil Rights laws were not passed to give civil rights protection to all Americans," but "out of a recognition that some Americans already had protection because they belong to a favored group; and others, including blacks, Hispanics, and women of all races, did not because they belonged to disfavored groups." The *New York Times,* 10 March 1985, E8. See also footnote 32 below.

[30]Friedman, "The New Black Intellectuals," 40. See also Thomas Sowell, *Race and Economics* (New York: David McKay, 1975) 218.

[31]Sowell, *Race and Economics,* 238.

[32]R. P. C. Hanson says that the West has "an ill-sorted collection of principles as a kind of individualistic, positivist, tolerant hedonism." Cited in *Context* (1 August 1984): 2. Some relate this to the aforementioned conservatism in general and with Ronald Reagan's leadership in particular. Rosalyn Carter, in a recent television interview, said that President Reagan has made people comfortable with their prejudices. Some observers are very concerned over the directions of the Justice Department's civil rights chief William Bradford Reynolds. "For

McCarthy says that money is "the newest pornography."

> How to get it, how to manipulate its institutions, how to make it grow, how to use it as an evergrowing source of power. Surely this is a reflection of the growing influence of greed as a motivating force in our society . . . The obsession with money may well run its course, but what will happen to our society in the meantime? . . . The love of money is far worse than the love of the flesh.[33]

Clearly, the pursuit of justice for minorities has to be supported by some measure of concern and goodwill on the part of the majority. Instead, the new generation of Preppies and Yuppies is looking out for Number One. One professor of business ethics was shocked to discover that some of his students supported racial discrimination because equality was a threat to their careers. This attitude of careerism and greed will have a negative effect on racial progress.

WHAT THE CHURCH CAN DO

An improper conclusion to the foregoing discussion is that nothing can be done to promote racial justice. While it may appear that Murphy's Law ("if anything can go wrong, it will") has captured the racial scene in the U.S., all is not lost. The community of faith has made a difference in this area in the past and can do so in the present and future. The difficulty arises as to proper goals and strategies. There are at least three possible views as to how the Church can be a part of the answer.

1. Some believe that the main contribution that the Church can make is to educate society about the enormous problems faced by minorities and encourage action to address these problems. This will bring about incremental changes. The view here is that, although the changes may be slow in coming, they will be solid and long-lasting. Consciousness raising will come as the result of speeches, writings, and promotion of movies and television programs that deal positively with racial issues. It is felt that racism is so deeply embedded that immediate changes are unlikely.

Donald Shriver suggests that one way the Church can educate is by revising history:

---

twenty-five years the Department of Justice has been viewed as a champion of Civil Rights. Today, it is viewed as an adversary," says Ralph Neas, executive director of the Leadership Conference on Civil Rights. "Uncivil Times at 'Justless,' " *Time* (13 May 1985): 58. A spokesperson of the American Civil Liberties Union said that "everything is exactly the opposite of what it's supposed to be." See also "A Right Turn on Race?" *Newsweek* (25 June 1984): 29.

[33]Abigail McCarty, "Lust and Money," *Commonweal* (March 26, 1982): 167.

Together, the black and feminist theologians both remind us that history always needs to be revised. This means welcoming an opportunity to read history emotionally and imaginatively through the eyes of Kunta Kinte and Chicken George, Harriet Tubman and Sojourner Truth. It means dwelling with curiosity on the mystery of how a church of black people came into being under the pressures of slavery, by what interior strength the black family survived slavery, the black church found nourishment in the ghetto, and the lures of an other-worldly hope spilled over into hope for this world. To read history morally is to ask how some things came to be that should not have been; how other things came to be in spite of much that hindered their being; and what things have yet to be, whose right to be must be asserted.[34]

It is important to transmit this history to the coming generation. Many young people of all races are ignorant of courageous and talented people in black history. They have no vision of the past.

2. Whereas those above favor education as the key to dealing with racial issues, others insist on a more activistic approach. These want to continue to form coalitions and press for immediate changes. Jesse Jackson, while believing in the importance of raising the consciousness of society, believes that change will come through organized efforts in the economic and political arenas. Marches, picketing, promoting minority candidates, and so forth, have lost some of their glow but are still considered an important avenue in promoting justice by those with an activistic bent.[35] Those concerned about racial issues are searching for ways to recapture the excitement and commitment of the Civil Rights Movement. Some fresh thinking along these lines is sorely needed. Shriver hopes that the churches will "work together on new patterns of racially comprehensive partnership."[36]

3. Another approach to the issue, promulgated by such ethicists as Stanley Hauerwas and John Howard Yoder,[37] may be referred to as the parabolic community approach. These believe that the Church can make its impact felt best by simply living out the gospel within the Church community. The Church can be a living parable, illustrating to the world that there is a better way. By

---

[34]Donald W. Shriver, Jr., "The Churches and the Future of Racism," *Theology Today* (July 1981): 153.

[35]It is interesting to note that the new Religious Right has adopted this approach to bring about the changes they desire. After centuries of virtual noninvolvement, some conservative Protestant groups have become radicalized, often endorsing candidates from the pulpit.

[36]Shriver, "The Churches," 155.

[37]Stanley Hauerwas, *A Community of Character* (Notre Dame: University Press, 1981) and *The Peaceable Kingdom* (Notre Dame: University Press, 1983). John Howard Yoder, *The Politics of Jesus* (Grand Rapids MI: Eerdmans, 1972) and *The Original Revolution* (Scottsdale PA: Herald Press, 1971).

exhibiting genuine agape love in an interracial Church, the Church fulfills its purpose and gives its witness to the world. The Church through its ministry promotes a vision of a new society, where people treat each other as brothers and sisters.

These three approaches are not necessarily mutually exclusive. Many Christians are comfortable in both the education and activist modes. The third model tends to reject the other two, sometimes seemingly out of frustration as well as conviction. It takes on some of the characteristics of Niebuhr's "Christ against Culture" model.[38] But in the arena of racial justice there is ample room for all people of goodwill. A diversity of approaches is both helpful and necessary. Commitment, courage, wisdom, and patience are needed most of all. It is a tall order.

---

[38]H. Richard Niebuhr, *Christ and Culture* (New York: Harper, 1951) Ch. 2.

CHRISTIAN LIFE-STYLE: TOWARD A RESPONSIBLE ECONOMIC ETHIC

DAVID R. WILKINSON
CHRISTIAN LIFE COMMISSION
SOUTHERN BAPTIST CONVENTION
NASHVILLE, TENNESSEE

INTRODUCTION

Jesus looking at him said, ''How hard it is for those who have riches to enter the kingdom of God! For it is easier for a camel to go through the eye of a needle than for a rich man to enter the kingdom of God.'' (Luke 18:24-25)[1]

Nearly two thousand years have come and gone since Jesus uttered those words. Yet they are just as shocking, just as radical, and just as relevant for today's audience as they were for the infamous ''rich young ruler'' and other members of the crowd that first heard Jesus' striking assertion. The relationship of material possessions to the Kingdom of God has challenged every generation of Christianity. Like the rich young ruler, every Christian must struggle with the question of how much is enough.

---

[1]All Scripture quotations are from the Revised Standard Version of the Bible, copyrighted 1946, 1952, 1971, 1973.

This question of economic life-style is crucial because it relates both directly and indirectly to a host of other social and moral issues.[2] It is fundamentally a question of ultimate loyalty, for, as Jesus stated forthrightly, one cannot serve both God and money.[3] Indeed, the teachings of Scripture, combined with the desperate needs of the world, ought to compel all Western Christians—particularly those who live in the United States of America—to reexamine their economic life-styles and to consider reducing their standards of living in order to adopt a simpler way of life.

WHY *SIMPLIFIED* LIFE-STYLE?

The call to voluntary simplicity, of course, is not new. Neither is it exclusive to Christianity. Philosophers, religious mystics, social prophets, environmentalists, back-to-nature idealists, and avoid-the-rat-race social dropouts have advocated the various practical, personal, spiritual, and social benefits of living simply. In recent decades, traditional arguments have been joined by some futurists, economists, and ecologists who believe the age of unrestrained consumption of the earth's resources has reached its peak and that simpler life-styles may become the necessary norm, even for the world's affluent minority. They have argued that uncontrollable factors such as depletion of inexpensive raw materials, critical energy shortages, pollution, economic crises, and changing balance of world power will force changes of life-styles in America and other developed nations.[4] While such dire warnings have faded during the recent preoccupation with ''economic recovery'' in America, they are bound to resurface in the face of unavoidable environmental and economic realities.

For the Christian, however, the issue of life-style is at root a theological issue, linked inseparably to the clear call of Christ and its ethical implications. As the Christian disciple considers questions of life-style, two introductory considerations are fundamental. First, it must be understood that, like poverty and wealth, life-style is a relative concept. There can be no legalistic

----

[2]Issues related to economics, including questions of personal and corporate life-style, have been addressed consistently and prophetically by T. B. Maston throughout his ministry of teaching and writing. While he has not specifically devoted a book to the subject, the issue of economic justice, perhaps as much as any particular ethical concern, interfaces at numerous points with the major themes of Maston's thought. Additionally, and just as importantly, Maston and his wife, Essie Mae, have given through the years quiet but tangible credibility to his teachings on biblical justice and Christian economics through the integrity of their own simple life-style.

[3]Matt. 6:24; Luke 16:13.

[4]Duane S. Elgin and Arnold Mitchell, ''Voluntary Simplicity: Lifestyle of the Future?'' *The Futurist* (August 1977): 206.

definition of how much is enough for every Christian in today's context. Neither the Bible nor Christian tradition prescribes a specific formula for economic life-style.

A second preliminary consideration is that American Christians must recognize that for most of us any *choice* about life-style is itself a luxury afforded by only a small minority of the world's people. Recorded in a penetrating magazine article several years ago, the reflections of Bailey King, a poor white Mississippi Southern Baptist, spoke eloquently about this luxury of choice:

> People's always tellin' us we got choices. Pore folks ain't got no choices. A choice is when two thangs is layin' there and you choose which one you want. If I had a choice, I wouldn't be living here.[5]

The undeniable truth is that billions of people—from rural counties in the American South to the barrios of Latin America to the refugee camps of Africa—have little or no options about life-style. Caught in the iron jaws of poverty and hunger, they struggle simply to exist. For them, survival is the *only* issue that greets each new sunrise. For them, "life-style" is a meaningless word.

With these two givens established, American Christians in particular are challenged by at least three overwhelming reasons to reduce their standards of living and to adopt simpler life-styles. First, we must live more simply because of limited global resources and their disproportionate consumption by the nations of the world. Every year this harsh reality becomes more evident and increasingly ominous. Many of the world's top scientists have warned that the earth cannot sustain current rates of consumption by the United States and other developed countries, due both to the depletion of resources and the disastrous effects of industrial pollution.

According to conservative estimates, the people of the United States require about thirty-three percent of the world's raw material production to gratify their needs. The authors of *The Limits of Growth,* a study published in 1972, estimated if the rest of the world were to attempt to live at the level of consumption within the United States, all known reserves of raw materials such as petroleum, tin, zinc, natural gas, copper, gold, lead, tungsten, and mercury would have disappeared entirely within ten years.[6] This threat is compounded by the effects of pollution, exorbitant costs for military production, and tremendous waste. Ecologists have wondered "whether we have already dug two-thirds of our way into an environmental grave."[7] In 1985,

---

[5]Phyllis F. Thompson, "Somebody a Poor Man," *Home Missions,* December 1979, 22.

[6]Donella H. Meadows et al., *The Limits to Growth* (New York: Signet Books, 1972) 64-67.

[7]Adam Daniel Finnerty, *No More Plastic Jesus* (New York: E. P. Dutton, 1978) 19.

the year that marked the fortieth anniversary of the atomic bomb, the nations of the world spent about one trillion dollars on military goods and services. The United States alone spent about one-third of that total.

Despite the numerous benefits—both real and contrived—of the free enterprise system, the U.S. remains ''the seat of a production and distribution system that is massively, staggeringly, wasteful. And it is designed to be that way.''[8] In light of such evidence, the unavoidable fact is that ''the world cannot afford our lifestyle; and . . . every year that we continue to live the way we do is another year of diminished resources and thus of diminished hope.''[9]

Meanwhile, the tremendous chasm between the rich and poor of the world, which geographically is primarily a North-South division, grows wider each year. America and the other highly developed nations of the world (Soviet Union, Japan, Canada, Western Europe) comprise less than thirty percent of the world's population. Yet this group possesses eighty percent of the world's income, consumes eighty-four percent of the earth's energy, and maintains a Gross National Product (sum of a country's goods and services produced in a year) that is fifteen times that of underdeveloped nations. One specialist has concluded that:

> differences in income per head between the poor and rich countries were around 1:2 at the beginning of the 19th century; they are around 1:40 today in nominal or around 1:20 in real terms.[10]

Such statistics indict American Christians, whose country marches at the head of the world's consumption parade.

The Christian, however, must confront such staggering statistics and dire predictions with an attitude of compassion and hope, grounded in a holistic, biblical theology of God and his relationship to the world. The view espoused by some Christians that a God who is in absolute control ''will always provide,'' so we should not worry about the depletion of natural resources, is at best a horribly naive theology and at worst a calloused, irresponsible distortion of Christianity. Likewise, the Christian ethic of *agape* love exposes the so-called ''lifeboat ethic'' as, in fact, an immoral, inhuman, and unchristian response to the global situation.[11] In contrast, Christians must adopt what

---

[8]Ibid., 31.

[9]Ibid., 18.

[10]James W. Howe et al., *The U.S. and World Development: Agenda for Action, 1975* (New York: Praeger, 1975) 166.

[11]See Garrett Hardin, ''Lifeboat Ethics: The Case Against Helping the Poor,'' *Psychology Today* 8:4 (September 1974): 38ff. See also William Paddock and Paul Paddock, *Famine 1975!* (Boston: Little, Brown and Co., 1967). For an excellent refutation of lifeboat ethics, see *Bread for the World Newsletter*, June 1976.

Carlyle Marney called an "ethic of parsimony," based on the assumption of the finiteness of creation.[12] Christian theology understands God as Creator and affirms the goodness in his creation. It recognizes that as Creator, God is Owner of everything; we are the caretakers, called by him into partnership as stewards of creation.

The God of creation is revealed in Scripture as a social Being who created human beings to live in relationship with him and with one another.[13] Furthermore, Christ's definition of one's neighbor demands an appreciation for the intricate network of interconnectedness within the human family.[14] The teachings of Scripture leave no room for isolationism or provincialism. We are global citizens, responsible *for* others and responsible *with* others for the quality of life on "spaceship earth."

POSSESSED OR POSSESSORS?

A second reason for living more simply is based upon an understanding of the burden of material possessions upon Christian discipleship and commitment. One of the hard-learned lessons of church history is that human beings easily become enslaved to the things they possess. Possessions have a way of becoming possessors. Many middle-class American Christians who fret about "all those bills" at the end of each month fail to recognize how the things in their lives have dictated the maintenance of a certain standard of living. One of the increasingly recognized plagues of modern technology is that it often robs people of their uniqueness and their humanity. To learn to live according to our needs rather than our wants is to increase the chances of freeing ourselves from the shackles of materialism and the impersonalization of a technological society. It is to be free of "the poverty of affluence."[15] If we are to "seek first his kingdom and his righteousness," then we must recognize and diligently avoid the inherent dangers of wealth.[16]

---

[12]Carlyle Marney, "The Ethics of Parsimony," *Proceedings* of 1977 Christian Life Commission seminar on the energy crisis.

[13]A theological understanding of the nature of God as a Person with moral and social attributes is foundational for Christian ethics, an emphasis found throughout T. B. Maston's writings. See, for example, the chapter on "The Nature of God," *Why Live the Christian Life?* (Nashville: Thomas Nelson, Inc., 1974).

[14]See Luke 10:29-37.

[15]Arthur G. Gish, *Beyond The Rat Race* (New Canaan CT: Keats Publishing, Inc., 1973) 19.

[16]Matt. 6:33.

The Bible does not teach that possessions are inherently evil. The Bible does teach that possessions are dangerous. They can distort values and confuse priorities. As T. B. Maston rightly perceived in one of his early works:

> The means of life tend to become the ends for which men live . . . material things, which should be instrumental and which should be used to promote spiritual ends, have become for millions of people the supreme values in life.[17]

Material possessions have the capacity to numb our concern for the poor and the oppressed and to contribute to their plight. One of the frightening things about the warnings of the Old Testament prophets and the teachings of Jesus is that the wealthy are condemned not merely for their direct oppression of the poor and powerless, but also for their simple neglect and unconcern. It should be remembered, for example, that the Pharisees of Jesus' day were meticulous about giving regularly to aid the poor. Yet the sin of the rich man in one of Jesus' parables was not direct abuse of the poor man Lazarus but his simple neglect for Lazarus's needs.[18]

In an interdependent world, Christians must understand that their lifestyles do have an impact on others. John Woolman, the Quaker saint of the eighteenth century, understood clearly this relationship between affluence and injustice. With a timeless insight, he saw that the "superfluities" and "luxuries" of the have's contributed to the suffering of the have-not's. He recognized the "love and ease of gain" as the underlying motive behind slavery and other social injustices of his day.[19] The same truth holds today. The slogan of the simple life-style movement, "live simply so that others may simply live" (adapted from Catholic saint Elizabeth Seton), rings simple but true. We must recognize that having more than enough can be a form of stealing from those in need. Materialism and over-indulgence, often baptized in the name of "progress," in reality make us accomplices in the violent crimes of hunger, poverty, and social injustice.

Wealth and possessions are dangerous because they are frequently sources of conflict between persons, groups, and nations. "What causes wars and what causes fighting among you?" asks the writer of James. "You desire and do not have; so you kill. And you covet and cannot obtain; so you fight and wage war."[20] Charles Wagner pointed out in his classic book, *The Simple Life,* that

---

[17]T. B. Maston, *World in Travail* (Nashville: Broadman Press, 1954) 95.

[18]Luke 16:19-31.

[19]John Woolman, *The Journal of John Woolman* in *The Doubleday Devotional Classics, Vol. III,* ed. E. Glenn Hinson, trans. Douglass Steere (Garden City NY: Doubleday and Co., Inc., 1978) 246.

[20]James 4:1-2.

"the more desires and needs a man has, the more occasion he finds for conflict with his fellowman."[21] Schumacher argued that "only by a reduction of needs can one promote a genuine reduction in those tensions that are the ultimate causes of strife and war."[22] Even a cursory review of world history confirms these views.

Additionally, possessions are seductive. They encourage covetousness, the desire for more and more material possessions, which dethrones God as the Lord of life. Jesus warned against this very danger: "Take heed, and beware of all covetousness; for a man's life does not consist in the abundance of his possessions."[23] Unfortunately, covetousness has become "a cardinal vice of Western civilization."[24] While I am not prepared to argue that capitalism is incompatible with Christianity, it must be admitted that many of capitalism's fundamental tenets encourage greed and acquisitiveness. The glorified profit motive is built into the system. According to one line in a short-lived Broadway musical, "If God says lovin' money is the root of all sin, Then God is unAmerican."[25] Southern Baptist ethicist James Dunn has declared that "the philosophy that fuels the money machine in Western life is a practical materialism. It is a materialism as damning as the materialism of Communism."[26] Christians must never forget that the sovereign God of the universe stands above any man-made economic system.

Living more simply encourages a healthy simplicity of attitude so desperately needed in a society that saps our spiritual vitality and resources. By freeing ourselves of the material, we can avoid what Wagner labeled the "artificial life."[27] We can learn to be human. A holy detachment from things, a carefree attitude toward possessions as taught by Jesus, encourages us to serve God with a singleness of purpose. It is a step toward being free, as Kierkegaard wrote, to pursue "purity of heart" by willing the Good only in our lives.[28] This attitude toward possessions, of course, has been one of the basic

---

[21]Charles Wagner, *The Simple Life* (New York: McClure, Phillips & Co., 1904) 7.

[22]E. F. Schumacher, *Small Is Beautiful* (New York: Harper & Row, 1973).

[23]Luke 12:15.

[24]Ron Sider, *Rich Christians in an Age of Hunger* (Downers Grove IL: Inter-Varsity Press, 1977) 123.

[25]Leonard Bernstein, *1600 Pennsylvania Avenue,* quoted by James M. Dunn in "A Christian Lifestyle for Twentieth Century Baptists."

[26]James M. Dunn, "A Christian Lifestyle for Twentieth Century Baptists," speech delivered at the Baptist World Alliance meeting, 1978, p. 4.

[27]Wagner, *The Simple Life,* 185.

[28]Soren Kierkegaard, *Purity of Heart* in *The Doubleday Devotional Classics, Vol. II,* ed. E. Glenn Hinson (Garden City NY: Doubleday and Co., Inc., 1978).

principles espoused by the great mystics of the Christian tradition, from St. Francis to Thomas Merton. It has undergirded the monastic movement in Roman Catholicism and the otherworldly tradition within Protestantism. Despite the extremes of monasticism, the truth remains that living more simply can be one means toward focusing on devotion to God alone. A simple lifestyle can be more than freedom *from* the dangers of material possessions; it can also be freedom *for* a deeper spiritual life with its subsequent benefits for individuals, families, church, and society. It can keep the spiritual springs flowing to supply the needed energy and discernment for effective Christian social action and redemptive ministry in the world.[29]

SIMPLIFIED LIFE-STYLE—MEANS OR AN END?

Thirdly, the Christian today must live more simply in order to *give* more freely. Indeed, without this vital element, simple life-style easily degenerates into mere asceticism. Voluntary simplicity must not be an end in itself, but a means to a greater end. Few people today experience the *joy* of giving through sacrificial self-denial that is part and parcel of the cross-like life taught by Scripture and modeled by Jesus.[30] With their traditional emphasis on tithing (and often the implicit assumption that ten percent is the maximum rather than the minimum requirement of Christian stewardship), Baptists have perhaps been just as legalistic (and perhaps less generous) than the Pharisees whom Jesus condemned for their lack of compassion for the poor and the downtrodden. Few of our real motivations for giving could withstand the penetrating judgment of the Light of the Gospel.

Yet there are at least two overwhelming needs in the world that should compel Christians to share: first, the injustice suffered by billions of persons hopelessly trapped by hunger and abject poverty, and second, the spiritual poverty of an estimated two and one-half billion persons who have never heard the Good News of the Gospel of Christ. Though there are many legitimate reasons for living simply in today's world, these twin concerns of justice and evangelism ought to be paramount for every evangelical Christian. This should be particularly true of Southern Baptists, who claim to be ''people of the Book'' with a cooperative fellowship grounded in a zeal for missions.

---

[29]For an excellent treatment of this important dimension, see Richard J. Foster, *Freedom of Simplicity* (New York: Harper & Row, 1981) and Foster, *Celebration of Discipline* (New York: Harper & Row, 1978).

[30]The cross as the ''unifying symbol'' of the Christian life represents one of T. B. Maston's most important contributions to Christian ethics. See *Why Live the Christian Life?*, 157-73.

The Lausanne Covenant, drawn up at the historic Lausanne Congress for World Evangelization in 1974, emphasized this two-pronged motivation for simpler life-styles:

> All of us are shocked by the poverty of millions and disturbed by the injustices which cause it. Those of us who live in affluent circumstances accept our duty to develop a simple lifestyle *in order to contribute generously to both relief and evangelism* (emphasis mine).[31]

Ron Sider has underscored this important point in a different way:

> Christians are *not* committed to a simple lifestyle. We are committed to Jesus Christ and his kingdom and thus to faithful participation in the mission of our servant King in a lost, broken world.[32]

WHOSE SIDE ARE YOU ON?

The biblical basis for a simplified life-style as a means of sharing with the poor and hungry has been documented thoroughly by Sider in *Rich Christians in an Age of Hunger*.[33] Likewise, there is little need to recite well-known statistics documenting the plight of more than one billion hungry and/or malnourished persons, most of whom live in Third and Fourth World countries. Through the mass media, we have been bombarded with images of starving children and impoverished families, especially during the tragic African famine of the mid-1980s. Indeed, part of the problem may be that our senses have been numbed by repeated exposure to such scenes. Identifying with the hungry of the world remains difficult for Americans and other well-fed, Western Christians.[34] In the midst of this insensitivity, the God of the Bible stands clearly on the side of the poor and the powerless. Evidence of this "bias" can be seen in the Exodus, the Exile, the Incarnation, and other pivotal points in revelation history.

Yet an honest evaluation of the place of most Americans in the global context forces us to admit that we must be numbered among the rich and powerful. Sider and other writers have driven home the point by posing in various ways the Bible's uncomfortable yet implicit question: If God is clearly on the

---

[31]"Lausanne Covenant," available from Lausanne Committee for World Evangelization, P.O. Box 1100, Wheaton, Il. 60187.

[32]Sider, ed., *Living More Simply* (Downers Grove IL: Inter-Varsity Press, 1980) 13.

[33]Sider, *Rich Christians in an Age of Hunger: A Biblical Study* (Downers Grove IL: Inter-Varsity Press, 1984, 2nd ed.).

[34]For an excellent illustration of how to identify with the poor, see the exercise suggested by Robert L. Heilbroner, *The Great Ascent: The Struggle for Economic Development in our Time* (New York: Harper & Row, 1963) 33-36.

side of the poor, and we Americans are among the rich, then whose side will we choose to be on? Despite lingering vestiges of the aversion to the so-called "social Gospel" among Southern Baptists and other Protestants, the weight of biblical evidence calls Christians to action in helping to alleviate the injustices of world hunger and systemic poverty.

Likewise, the Christian call to evangelism and missions requires sacrificial giving. While worldwide missions has been the flag around which Southern Baptists have rallied since 1845, the fact remains that missions in the largest Protestant denomination in the world has largely lived off the fat. If an economic downturn should force missions to survive on sacrifice rather than surplus, denominational themes such as Bold Mission Thrust could soon become empty slogans. As Cecil Ray has argued:

> Lifestyle choices set the limits of mission support. Only a limited survey is required to determine that we are near the limit of mission support growth within our existing lifestyle values. . . . If no limit is set on the appetite for things, there is little hope. Where this line is drawn determines what is available for mission support—for missions lives on what is left.[35]

STEPS TOWARD CHRISTIAN LIFE-STYLE

If one accepts these arguments for adopting simplified life-styles, an immediate question, of course, is where or how to begin. As indicated earlier, any specific response is difficult because of broad parameters of personal response and the relative nature of simple life-style. As one considers the quest, however, he or she should be reminded of several preliminary warnings.

First, the approach to the life-style advocated here requires intellectual and spiritual honesty in interpreting Scripture. This is vital, for a proper foundation must be laid before major changes are attempted. Too often Christians have been guilty of erecting subtle, often sophisticated, detours around the radical demands of the Bible, particularly the "hard sayings" of Jesus.[36] Jesus, for instance, had more to say about our attitude toward possessions than "salvation." The Synoptic Gospels speak more of wealth and poverty than they do of heaven and hell. One in ten New Testament verses relates to money and its use.[37] Yet we often take the sting out of the Bible's harsh teachings by rationalizing or spiritualizing them.

---

[35]Cecil Ray, "Lifestyle: Friend or Foe of Mission Support?", unpublished paper, 1979.

[36]See Don Kraybill, "Detours Around Jesus," *The Other Side* (December 1978): 17-21.

[37]Dunn, "A Christian Lifestyle," 2.

Theologians and biblical scholars, of course, have differed in their interpretations of the teachings of Jesus. But in the midst of such diversity of opinion, the call to live more simply asks only that Jesus be taken *seriously*.

The call to simple life-style is a plea for *radical* discipleship; it has nothing to do with being "liberal" or "conservative." (Indeed, it is my contention that many of those who have clamored most noisily about devotion to the Bible—with such catchwords as the "inerrancy" of Scripture—have been noticeably silent about the Bible's teachings on economics and justice for the poor and the oppressed.)

Perhaps the first step in an honest approach to Scripture is to resist the temptation to think only in terms of "them" when confronted by demanding teachings related to money, wealth, and possessions. We must recognize that biblical injunctions concerning the rich and powerful may very well be addressed to *us*. We would do well to remember with C. S. Lewis that:

All things (e.g. a camel's journey through A
    needle's eye) are possible, it's true;
But picture how the camel feels, squeezed out
    In one long bloody thread from tail to snout.[38]

Secondly, we must avoid the tendency to confuse "the American Way" with God's way, the United States flag with the cross of Christ, and laissez-faire economics with God's will. This attitude creeps quietly into our theology and cleverly colors our reading of Scripture. The assumption that the American way is synonymous with God's way finds expression in numerous pulpits every Sunday. It enjoys support in the uncritical allegiance to the Protestant work ethic and many of the built-in assumptions of the economics of Adam Smith. Society acts as though self-aggrandizement is a God-given right. Billions of dollars are spent each year by the advertising industry in polished attempts to convince us that Jesus was grossly mistaken about the rightful place of possessions. The fact is that the Kingdom of God stands above any earthly economic system, including capitalism.

The Christian who opts to live more simply will confront culture—and, indeed, much of the acculturated, contemporary church—head on. As Maston pointed out more than twenty years ago, the sad truth is that "many of our churches are little more than cultural institutions. They tend not only to identify themselves with the culture, but to become defenders of that culture."[39] Unfortunately, in a day when civil religion rules too many pulpits,

---

[38]C. S. Lewis, *Poems*, ed. Walter Hooper (New York: Harcourt Brace Jovanovich, 1977) 134.

[39]Maston, "Christian Living and the Way Ahead," *Quarterly Review* (January-March 1965): 48.

"the rhetoric of the American way has become so sacred in the minds of many Christians that it is dangerous to challenge it."[40]

Finally, simplified life-style must beware the trap of legalistic asceticism. Living simply is not an escape from the world, but a call to redemptive action in the world. The call to simplicity does not represent an aversion to material things, but rather affirms the goodness of God's creation. It is not a wholesale condemnation of material possessions; nor is it a naive glorification of poverty as the biblical ideal. Neither does living more simply exclude the need for the aesthetic. Rather, it recognizes that "pleasure and simplicity are two old acquaintances."[41] Any attempt to propose a simple formula for simple living is to ignore the necessary complexities involved and to destroy the spirit exemplified by Christ.

With this limitation in mind, the practical suggestions that follow are offered only as possible guidelines in response to the question of how to begin to live more simply. The hope is that they will stimulate other practical guidelines for implementing the biblical call to faithful stewardship.[42]

1. With a reliance upon Scripture and prayer, seek to make a distinction between needs and wants. "We need to distinguish between necessities and luxuries and normally reject both our desire for the latter and our inclination to blur the distinction."[43] Subject family or individual decisions about acquiring things to the light of Scripture and the guidance of the Holy Spirit through prayer. Keep in mind the larger context of the global Christian community.

2. Eat sensibly and eat less. Americans have among the most wasteful diets in the world. We eat, for example, two to four times as much meat as the body can use.

3. Consume less energy. Drive less and walk more. Cut down on unnecessary trips. Turn the thermostat down in the winter and up in the summer. Maintain appliances and keep them until they wear out—not until a shiny new model comes out.

4. Consider adopting what many have called a Just World Standard of Living, a life-style that everyone in the world could share without rapidly depleting the earth's natural resources and provoking ecological disaster.

---

[40]Dunn, "A Christian Lifestyle," 4.

[41]Wagner, *The Simple Life*, 95.

[42]For further suggestions on practical approaches to living more simply, see Arthur Gish, *Beyond The Rat Race;* and Ron Sider, *Lifestyle in the Eighties* (Philadelphia: Westminster Press, 1982); *Living More Simply;* and *99 Ways to a Simple Lifestyle* (New York: Anchor Press/Doubleday, 1977).

[43]Ron Sider, "Implementing the Right to Food," *Proceedings* from Southern Baptist Convocation on World Hunger, 1978, p. 49.

5. Consider the "graduated tithe" or a similar concept as a pattern for giving that will enable you to free resources to share with others.[44]

6. Fast regularly or skip at least one meal each week. Give the money saved to world hunger relief. Use the time saved for prayer, meditation, study, and other means of spiritual renewal.

7. Dress modestly. Resist the temptation to keep up with the latest clothing fashions. Avoid the Madison Avenue syndrome by wearing clothes until they wear out.

8. Practice informed Christian citizenship. Become knowledgeable about government policies that have an impact on foreign aid, military spending, food policy, and overseas development.

9. Explore creative ways of celebrating special occasions more simply. Rebel against cultural prostitution of Christian celebrations such as Christmas and Easter.

10. Help lead your church to adopt a corporate life-style consistent with biblical teachings about the Christian's responsibility for the poor and the oppressed. Priorities should focus on people rather than buildings and budgets. Emphasize the New Testament model of "economic koinonia" as found in Acts 2.

CONCLUSION

To adopt a responsible life-style consistent with the highest calling of Christian discipleship requires a deep reservoir of spiritual and emotional resources from which to draw strength and wisdom. The Christian who attempts to live more simply will confront obstacles at every turn in the journey, a reminder of the fundamental tension that is both "natural and inevitable for the serious Christian."[45] Consequently, spiritual maturity is essential. Far too many idealistic crusaders have "burned out" or fallen into empty despair because they lacked the spiritual depth and maturity to implement their lofty ideas. In addition, bucking culture, as a simplified life-style inevitably must do in today's consumption-oriented American society, is a challenge that is virtually impossible to accomplish alone. Here the mutual commitment, support, and love of the fellowship of faith is crucial. The questions of life-style should be addressed within the corporate context of *koinonia*. Economic considerations should benefit from the wisdom of others. Likewise, decisions

---

[44]This concept is explained by Sider in *Rich Christians*, 166-69 (Rev. Ed.). Among Southern Baptists, a similar proposal has been incorporated into a renewed emphasis on cooperative missions support in Cecil Ray and Susan Ray, *Cooperation: The Baptist Way to a Lost World* (Nashville: Stewardship Commission of the Southern Baptist Convention, 1985).

[45]Maston, *Why Live the Christian Life?*, 174.

about life-style should be called into accountability by loving, fellow pilgrims.

This support is vital, for the demands of Scripture are hauntingly clear. The writer of 1 John puts it bluntly:

> If anyone has the world's goods and sees his brother in need, yet closes his heart against him, how does God's love abide in him? Little children, let us not love in word or speech but in deed and truth.[46]

---

[46]1 John 3:17-18.